McGraw-Hill
GED

Language Arts, Reading

WORKBOOK

*The Most Thorough Practice for
the GED Test*

John M. Reier

McGraw·Hill

New York   Chicago   San Francisco   Lisbon   London   Madrid   Mexico City
Milan   New Delhi   San Juan   Seoul   Singapore   Sydney   Toronto

Printed in the United States of America.

8 9 0   QDB/QDB   15 14 13 12

ISBN 0-07-140711-1

McGraw-Hill books are available at special quantity discounts to use as premiums and sales promotions, or for use in corporate training programs. For more information, please write to the Director of Special Sales, Professional Publishing, McGraw-Hill, Two Penn Plaza, New York, NY 10121-2298. Or contact your local bookstore.

This book is printed on acid-free paper.

Table of Contents

Acknowledgments

Excerpt on page 4 from "Giving Children a Good Start" by Carol Emig, as appeared in *Chicago Tribune,* December 12, 1986. Reprinted by permission of the author.

Excerpt on page 6 from *Overcoming Math Anxiety, Revised and Expanded Edition* by Sheila Tobias. Copyright © 1993, 1978 by Sheila Tobias. Used by permission of W. W. Norton & Company, Inc.

Excerpt on page 8 from a speech, "An American Prisoner of War," by James N. Rowe, as appeared in *Contemporary American Speeches,* 9e, 2000, by Kendall Hunt. Reprinted by permission of Wil Linkugel.

Excerpt on page 12 from *How To Look At Dance* by Walter Terry. Text copyright © 1982 by Walter Terry, photographs copyright © 1982 by Jack and Linda Vartoogian. Reprinted by permission of HarperCollins Publishers Inc.

Excerpt on page 13 reprinted from *HRnext.com,* with permission of the publisher, Business and Legal Reports, Inc.

Excerpt on page 14 reprinted from *HRnext.com,* with permission of the publisher, Business and Legal Reports, Inc.

Excerpt on page 16 reprinted from *HRnext.com,* with permission of the publisher, Business and Legal Reports, Inc.

Excerpt on page 18 from *The Right Stuff* by Tom Wolfe. Copyright © 1979 by Tom Wolfe. Reprinted by permission of Farrar, Straus and Giroux, LLC.

Excerpt on page 24 from "Gas Station," from *The Oranging of America* by Max Apple, copyright © 1974,1975, 1976 by Max Apple. Used by permission of Viking Penguin, a division of Penguin Putnam Inc.

Excerpt on page 27 from book review, "Supreme Insult." Copyright © 1986 by Conde Nast Publications Inc. All rights reserved. Originally published in *Vogue,* October 1986. Reprinted by permission.

Excerpt on page 32 from "Crime Does Pay" by Sid Smith, *Chicago Tribune,* November 16, 1986. Reprinted by permission of the Chicago Tribune.

Excerpt on page 34 from "The New High-Style Hospital" by Douglas Davis, *Newsweek,* July 28. © 1986 Newsweek, Inc. All rights reserved. Reprinted by permission.

Excerpt on page 35 from *Six Black Masters of American Art* by Romare Bearden and Harry Henderson. © Romare Bearden Foundation/Licensed by VAGA, New York, NY. Reprinted by permission.

Excerpt on page 36 from "Shedd Shows American Folk Art at its Best" by Jay Pridmore, as appeared in *Chicago Tribune,* November 14, 1986, copyright Jay Pridmore. Reprinted by permission of the author.

Excerpt on page 38 from "The Untold Lie," in *Winesburg, Ohio* by Sherwood Anderson. Copyright 1919 by B.W. Huebsch; Copyright 1947 by Eleanor Copenhaver Anderson. Used by permission of Viking Penguin, a division of Penguin Putnam Inc.

Excerpt on page 42 from "Charles" in *The Lottery* by Shirley Jackson. Copyright © 1948, 1949 by Shirley Jackson. Reprinted by permission of Farrar, Straus and Giroux, LLC.

Excerpt on page 44 adapted from *Savior, Savior, Hold My Hand* by Piri Thomas. Reprinted by permission of the author.

Excerpt on page 45 from "A Summer's Reading," from *The Magic Barrel* by Bernard Malamud. Copyright © 1950, 1958, renewed 1977, 1986 by Bernard Malamud. Reprinted by permission of Farrar, Straus and Giroux, LLC.

Excerpt on page 46 from "Tony's Story" by Leslie Marmon Silko, in *Storyteller.* Copyright © 1981 by Leslie Marmon Silko, reprinted with the permission of The Wylie Agency, Inc.

Excerpt on page 48 reprinted with permission of Simon & Schuster, from *Terms of Endearment* by Larry McMurtry. Copyright © 1975 by Larry McMurtry.

Poem on page 53, "Poem," excerpted from *So Going Around Cities: New & Selected Poems* 1958–1979, copyright © 1980 by Ted Berrigan. Reprinted by permission of Blue Wind Press.

Poem on page 54, "P.S. 42" by Gregory Corso from *Long Live Man,* copyright © 1962 by Gregory Corso. Reprinted by permission of New Directions Corp.

Introduction

Welcome to *McGraw-Hill's GED Language Arts, Reading Workbook*. This book will help you prepare for the GED Language Arts, Reading Test. There are four main sections in this exercise book: Nonfiction Prose, Prose Fiction, Poetry, and Drama. Each section gives you additional practice in an area covered in McGraw-Hill's main reading textbook, *GED Language Arts, Reading*. The organization of this workbook parallels that of the main textbook, so if you need a review or further instruction, refer to our main reading text.

This workbook also contains a full-length GED practice test. This test is similar to the actual GED Language Arts, Reading Test. It's the same length as the GED Test, and it's in the same format.

Content Areas

The passages on the GED Language Arts, Reading Test are taken from the following content areas:

- Literary Text

- Nonfiction Text

The literary text selections are taken from the works of recognized authors, both recent and past. Their work includes prose fiction (excerpts from novels, short stories, and folk tales), poetry, and excerpts from plays. Nonfiction writers such as journalists, essayists, and newspaper reporters produce the selections for nonfiction text. These sections include reviews, essays, articles, speeches, biographies, business documents, and articles about the visual arts.

The GED Language Arts, Reading Test consists of seven passages or excerpts. Of those passages, 75% come from literary text, and 25% come from nonfiction sources.

The passages from Literary Text include three types of literature:

Prose Fiction

Imagined events, characters, and places are the topics of fictional prose. Examples of fictional prose include short stories and novels. Three of the seven passages on the GED Language Arts, Reading Test will be examples of Prose Fiction. One passage will come from each of these three literary time periods:

- Before 1920

- 1920–1960

- After 1960

Poetry

In poetry the sounds and arrangement of words produce a rhythmic, or musical, effect. Sentences are divided into lines, and the language is condensed. The person telling the poem is called the *speaker*. One passage will be a poetry selection.

Drama

Drama is written in script form, consisting primarily of dialogue and stage directions. Playwrights write their plays so that actors can perform them. In addition to the characters' words, the stage directions tell us how the playwright wants the actors to perform the play. One passage will be a drama selection.

Two of the seven passages on the GED Language Arts, Reading Test will be from Nonfiction Text.

Passages from Nonfiction Text are about real people, places, events, and social issues. Therefore, the purpose of these reading selections is to present factual information or to express a viewpoint. Examples of nonfiction prose include newspaper and magazine articles, essays, speeches, biographies, and business documents.

Reading Skills

The GED Language Arts, Reading Test consists of seven passages followed by a set of multiple-choice questions. In all, there are forty questions on the test. Your ability to answer these questions correctly requires you to master the following basic reading skills:

Comprehension
- Identifying the directly stated main idea—the sentence that expresses the major point of the passage
- Recognizing supporting details—directly stated examples, facts, descriptions, or reasons

Application
- Applying information and ideas to a new context or situation

Analysis
- Examining the author's use of language and its effects
- Locating clues that suggest the unstated main idea
- Drawing conclusions from supporting details
- Interpreting figurative language—using context clues to determine a meaning that words or phrases suggest beyond the literal level

Synthesis
- Determining how and why an author organizes information
- Interpreting the tone, point of view, or purpose of a passage
- Linking elements of a passage
- Integrating information from outside a passage with information from within the passage (extended synthesis)

At the beginning of each chapter in this exercise book, you'll see references to text pages. These page numbers refer to *McGraw-Hill's GED Language Arts, Reading* as well as the complete *McGraw-Hill's GED*. Refer to the appropriate pages in these books whenever you need to review.

The following table presents the percentage of questions that you will be asked in each of these reading skills.

Reading Skill	Percentage of the Test Questions	
Comprehension	20%	(8 questions)
Application	15%	(6 questions)
Analysis	30–35%	(12–14 questions)
Synthesis	30–35%	(12–14 questions)

The Purpose Question
You will notice that a brief question precedes each passage. This is called a *purpose question*. The purpose question draws your attention to the content of the passage. Remember, however, that the purpose question is not the title of the selection. Use the purpose question as a study aid to focus your reading.

Chapter 1

Nonfiction Prose

GED Language Arts, Reading pages 109–164
Complete GED pages 655–684

The passages in this chapter are all examples of Nonfiction Prose. Study the following passages and answer the multiple-choice questions. Use the purpose questions to focus your reading.

Informational Nonfiction

Passages on Informational Nonfiction will include business documents, speeches, newspaper and magazine articles, and research reports.

Questions 1–5 are based on the following passage.

WHAT ACTIONS ARE CONSIDERED CRIMINAL?

The laws of each state determine what is considered a crime. In one state, driving over 70 miles an hour may be a crime, while in another, 60 is the limit. Buying alcohol
5 may be a crime in one state and not in another. Crime varies with time as well as place. Thus, in colonial America, failure to attend church was a crime, as was participation in witchcraft. Today, these are
10 no longer crimes.

In general, there are two kinds of crimes. Felonies, which include murder, robbery, and arson (deliberately setting something afire), are the most serious. Anyone who commits
15 a felony can be sent to a state prison for a year or more; in some states certain felonies carry the death penalty. Misdemeanors are less serious; the penalty is a fine or imprisonment of up to a year in jail.
20 Shoplifting, driving while drunk, and stealing money and goods worth less than $50 are examples of misdemeanors. In cases where it is not clear whether the crime is a felony or a misdemeanor, it is a judge who makes
25 the final decision. Crimes may also be classified as being against persons or against property. Crimes against persons include assault, murder, and kidnapping; property crimes include burglary, robbery,
30 and auto theft.

—Excerpted from *Crime and Juvenile Delinquency*
by Gerald Leinwald

1. Which of the following best describes an arsonist?

   A person who
   (1) damages public property
   (2) accidentally starts a fire
   (3) intentionally burns property
   (4) serves a long prison term
   (5) commits a serious crime

2. Which statement best summarizes the main idea of the first paragraph?

   (1) Driving over the speed limit is a crime.
   (2) Today, unfair laws no longer exist.
   (3) Practicing witchcraft in colonial America was illegal.
   (4) Crime varies with time and place.
   (5) Laws requiring church attendance have been abolished.

3. Who or what determines what type of behavior is a crime?

   (1) police officers
   (2) state laws
   (3) attorneys
   (4) jury members
   (5) felonies

4. What is the author's purpose in the second paragraph?

   To explain
   (1) the process of enforcing the law
   (2) the causes of criminal behavior
   (3) the effects of judges' decisions
   (4) the difference between theft and murder
   (5) the classifications of crime

5. Which of the following people would most likely be committing a misdemeanor?

   (1) a mugger
   (2) a shoplifter
   (3) a drug dealer
   (4) an arsonist
   (5) a spy

Questions 6–10 are based on the following passage.

WHAT SOCIAL PROBLEM CONCERNS THE AUTHOR?

So many issues now receiving attention in the media and on the political [agenda] are really family issues—drug abuse, teen suicide, teen pregnancy, the crisis in
5 education. If we can redirect our discussions of these issues to an exploration of what can be done early in a child's life to help families create a healthy environment in which to grow and develop, we can lessen both the
10 likelihood and the extent of many subsequent personal and societal crises.

We place great stock in the importance and effectiveness of preventative measures, and research and practical experience are
15 behind us. We know, for example, that:

Children who do not receive regular preventive health care from an early age are likely to suffer from undetected health problems and disabilities.

20 Children without supportive adult care are likely to lack confidence, feel alienated and distrustful and suffer from learning and behavioral problems.

Children who are not stimulated and
25 encouraged to develop through activities appropriate to their age are likely to experience problems in school.

While parents rightfully bear the primary responsibility for children in this society,
30 government policies and the policies, practices and attitudes of major institutions—the workplace, the community, the school, the health care system, the courts—profoundly affect the extent to
35 which parents can provide their children with a good start.

—Excerpted from *Caring for America's Children*
by Carol A. Emig

6. What major issue does the author discuss in this passage?

   (1) drug abuse
   (2) family environment
   (3) teen pregnancy
   (4) crises in education
   (5) teen suicide

7. According to the author, who bears the primary responsibility for children in this society?

   (1) academic institutions
   (2) the government
   (3) the community
   (4) parents
   (5) the health care system

8. Which of the following suggestions would the author be *least* likely to support?

   (1) Employers should fire workers who occasionally stay home to care for their young children.
   (2) Neighborhood organizations should sponsor youth recreation centers.
   (3) Schools should hire psychologists trained in diagnosing learning disabilities.
   (4) More corporations should consider establishing in-house day-care centers.
   (5) Affordable counseling should be made available to low-income families.

9. According to the passage, which of the following conclusions is valid?

   (1) Children raised in caring environments don't develop medical problems.
   (2) Single parents ignore their children's emotional needs.
   (3) Girls who feel alienated will eventually become unwed mothers.
   (4) A responsible, understanding father can increase his child's self-esteem.
   (5) Children who play with toy guns will display hostility in school.

10. What technique does the author use to analyze the topic?

    (1) descriptive details
    (2) cause-and-effect relationships
    (3) comparison and contrast
    (4) step-by-step instructions
    (5) classification

Questions 11–15 are based on the following passage.

WHY ARE SOME PEOPLE AFRAID OF MATH?

The first thing people remember about failing at math is that it felt like sudden death. Whether the incident occurred while learning "word problems" in sixth grade,
5 coping with equations in high school, or first confronting calculus and statistics in college, failure came suddenly and in a very frightening way. An idea or a new operation was not just difficult, it was impossible! And,
10 instead of asking questions or taking the lesson slowly, most people remember having had the feeling that they would never go any further in mathematics. If we assume that the curriculum was reasonable, and that
15 the new idea was but the next in a series of learnable concepts, the feeling of utter defeat was simply not rational; yet "math anxious" college students and adults have revealed that no matter how much the
20 teacher reassured them, they could not overcome that feeling.

A common myth about the nature of mathematical ability holds that one either has or does not have a mathematical mind.
25 Mathematical imagination and an intuitive grasp of mathematical principles may well be needed to do advanced research, but why should people who can do college-level work in other subjects not be able to do
30 college-level math as well? Rates of learning may vary. Competency under time pressure may differ. Certainly low self-esteem will get in the way. But where is the evidence that a student needs a "mathematical mind" in
35 order to succeed at learning math?

—Excerpted from *Overcoming Math Anxiety*
by Sheila Tobias

11. Why does the author compare people's memories of failing math to "sudden death" (lines 2–3)?

(1) Their teachers threatened to flunk them.
(2) They considered committing suicide.
(3) They felt panicky and defeated.
(4) They hadn't prepared for the test.
(5) They expected a higher grade.

12. Which of the following people require the most math training to perform their jobs?

(1) librarians
(2) novelists
(3) bank tellers
(4) engineers
(5) waiters

13. According to the author, what is a common myth about learning math?

(1) Low self-esteem interferes with a student's progress.
(2) Rates of learning vary among individuals.
(3) Some students are more sensitive to time pressures.
(4) Only people born with mathematical talent succeed in math.
(5) Teachers can help students to overcome mental blocks.

14. What should students do if they have difficulty solving a new math problem?

(1) work quickly
(2) become anxious
(3) ask for reassurance
(4) skip the problem
(5) ask questions

15. Which word best describes the author's approach to writing the passage?

(1) analytical
(2) persuasive
(3) descriptive
(4) irrational
(5) impersonal

Questions 16–20 are based on the following passage.

WHAT DID ABRAHAM LINCOLN SAY IN THE GETTYSBURG ADDRESS?

Four score and seven years ago our fathers brought forth on this continent a new nation, conceived in liberty and dedicated to the proposition that all men are created equal.

5 Now we are engaged in a great civil war, testing whether that nation, or any nation so conceived and so dedicated, can long endure. We are met on a great battlefield of that war. We have come to dedicate a
10 portion of that field as a final resting place for those who here gave their lives that that nation might live. It is altogether fitting and proper that we should do this.

But in a larger sense we cannot
15 dedicate, we cannot consecrate, we cannot hallow this ground. The brave men, living and dead, who struggled here, have consecrated it far above our poor power to add or detract. The world will little note nor
20 long remember what we say here, but it can never forget what they did here. It is for us, the living, rather, to be dedicated here to the unfinished work which they who fought here have thus far so nobly advanced. It is
25 rather for us to be here dedicated to the great task remaining before us—that from these honored dead we take increased devotion to that cause for which they gave the last full measure of devotion; that we
30 here highly resolve that these dead shall not have died in vain; that this nation, under God, shall have a new birth of freedom; and that government of the people, by the people, for the people, shall not perish from
35 the earth.

—"The Gettysburg Address" by Abraham Lincoln

16. What is Lincoln's main reason for delivering this speech?

   (1) to pay tribute to the soldiers who died at Gettysburg
   (2) to blame the South for dividing the nation
   (3) to restate the principles of the Declaration of Independence
   (4) to explain why heroic action is more memorable than words
   (5) to encourage the North to defeat the South

17. What can you infer that the phrase "final resting place" (line 10) means?

   (1) a nation
   (2) a barracks
   (3) a field
   (4) a cemetery
   (5) a battleground

18. According to the speech, what is Lincoln's political goal?

   (1) to abolish slavery
   (2) to punish the South
   (3) to preserve democracy
   (4) to prove America's religious devotion
   (5) to proclaim the soldiers as heroes

19. Which of the following words does *not* accurately describe the writing style of "The Gettysburg Address?"

   (1) inspirational
   (2) impersonal
   (3) direct
   (4) concise
   (5) sincere

20. The speaker before Lincoln spoke for two hours, and his speech is not remembered. Lincoln spoke for two minutes and gave one of the most memorable speeches in history.

What can you infer made Lincoln's speech memorable?

   (1) its emphasis on the victory
   (2) its understanding of the occasion
   (3) its long list of quotations
   (4) its reference to the losing side
   (5) its rambling and distortion

Questions 21–25 are based on the following passage.

WHAT DOES MAJOR ROWE EXPRESS IN HIS SPEECH?

The American prisoners of war are particularly close to those of us in the military, because the prisoners of war are members of military. It could be any one of
5   us, and I was one of those prisoners of war. I am Major Nick Rowe; I spent 62 months as a prisoner of the Viet Cong in South Vietnam. The issue of the prisoners of war has come to the forefront in our nation; and in
10   bringing this issue to the forefront, we have found that it's not that American people don't remember, or that they don't care, it's that most of the people in our country don't know. And those of us who have come out
15   feel that we have a particular duty, because we are speaking for 1,600 men who have no voices. So this afternoon I would like to bring you some insight into the prison camps and some insight into what an
20   American prisoner of war lives through.

I was a Special Forces advisor in 1963 in Phuoc Hoa. I was in a camp approximately in this area and was captured very near there in October of 1963. Shortly after capture, I
25   was moved down in the Mekong region; I stayed in this region until January of 1965, when I was moved into the U Minh Forest. I stayed in the U Minh Forest from January 1965 through December of 1968, when I
30   escaped. The camp I was held in was on canal 21 and canal 6. I was approximately fourteen kilometers from our old district capital. I was that close to Americans, and yet they couldn't get to me nor could I get
35   to them. This is the most frustrating thing about being an American prisoner in South Vietnam.

—Excerpted from *An American Prisoner of War in South Vietnam* by James M. Rowe

21. What is the main topic of the speech?

  (1) a history of Major Rowe's military career
  (2) the American public's insight into the Vietnam War
  (3) prison camps and an American prisoner-of-war's experience
  (4) the way the media reported the Vietnam War
  (5) South Vietnamese methods for capturing prisoners

22. Why is Major Rowe especially qualified to deliver this speech?

  (1) He served his duty as a Special Forces advisor.
  (2) He spent 62 months as a prisoner of the Viet Cong.
  (3) He has already brought the issue to the forefront.
  (4) He personally interviewed 1,600 prisoners of war.
  (5) He has the rank of an officer in the military.

23. In what year did Major Rowe escape?

  (1) 1961
  (2) 1962
  (3) 1963
  (4) 1965
  (5) 1968

24. Which word best describes the speech's tone?

  (1) straightforward
  (2) sarcastic
  (3) outraged
  (4) complicated
  (5) distorted

25. With what other situation can Major Rowe's experience best be compared?

  (1) American military involvement in Central America
  (2) American citizens held hostage in a foreign country
  (3) World War II soldiers fighting the Nazis
  (4) an American soldier imprisoned for treason against the United States
  (5) Americans protesting the Vietnam War

Questions 26–30 are based on the following passage.

WHAT DO YOU LEARN ABOUT AMERICAN INDIAN MUSIC?

To the Europeans, the rhythms and melodies of Indian music were unfamiliar and pagan, not easily appreciated when compared to their own kind of music. Some
5 of the Indian music does indeed have a mysterious, almost hypnotic quality that can cast a sort of spell over the listener.

All of the songs of the Indians had a purpose. They did not sing or play their
10 instruments for audiences. Rather, they sang to their spirits—asking for help or giving thanks. To the Indians, singing and music were not considered as performances but as part of life itself. There was a song for every
15 ceremony or special occasion and also for marking all of the important steps in an individual's life. It was not unusual for an Indian to know several hundred songs and to be able to repeat each one of them
20 perfectly.

Some of the songs were made by man: that is, they were deliberately created in his mind or his thoughts. They were sung to please the ear while at the same time
25 expressing feelings. They stirred Indians to perform great deeds in hunting or in war, giving them strength to meet danger, to endure pain, and to face death bravely. But most songs originated in dreams or visions.
30 Because the Indians believed they came from a supernatural source, they had great powers and were considered holy. Such a song became the Indian's personal property. The person owned not only the song but
35 also its powers and no one else could sing it without the owner's permission. Sometimes the Indian would sell the right to sing the song to someone who especially liked the words and the power it commanded.

—Excerpted from *American Indian Music and Musical Instruments* by George S. Fichter

26. How would the Europeans probably characterize Indian music?

    (1) spellbinding
    (2) unfamiliar
    (3) mysterious
    (4) captivating
    (5) rhythmic

27. Indian songs can best be compared to which of the following?

    (1) prayers
    (2) popular music
    (3) poetry
    (4) greeting cards
    (5) news bulletins

28. Which of the following statements best expresses the main idea of the second paragraph?

    (1) Indians didn't perform their songs for an audience.
    (2) Indians created songs for ceremonies and special occasions.
    (3) Many Indians knew several hundred songs.
    (4) Indians learned to memorize their favorite songs.
    (5) All of the Indian songs had a purpose.

29. Based on the passage, what can you conclude that Indian music is *not*?

    (1) spiritual
    (2) creative
    (3) emotional
    (4) commercial
    (5) inspirational

30. What is the author's main purpose in writing this passage?

    (1) to rate the skills of Indian musicians
    (2) to persuade readers to buy CDs
    (3) to inform the reader about the music's cultural function
    (4) to analyze the technical characteristics of Indian music
    (5) to compare Indian music to European music

Questions 31–36 are based on the following passage.

WHAT DOES A REPORTER OBSERVE ABOUT THE SAN FRANCISCO EARTHQUAKE?

The earthquake in San Francisco shook down hundreds of thousands of dollars' worth of walls and chimneys. But the conflagration that followed burned up hundreds of millions
5 of dollars' worth of property. There is no estimating within hundreds of millions the actual damage wrought.

Not in history has a modern imperial city been so completely destroyed. San
10 Francisco is gone. Nothing remains of it but memories and a fringe of dwelling houses on its outskirts. Its industrial section is wiped out. Its business section is wiped out. Its social and residential section is wiped out.
15 The factories and warehouses, the great stores and newspaper buildings, the hotels and the palaces … are all gone. There only remains the fringe of dwelling-houses on the outskirts of what was once San Francisco.

20 Within an hour after the earthquake shock, the smoke of San Francisco's burnings was a lurid tower visible a hundred miles away. And for three days and nights the lurid tower swayed in the sky, reddening
25 the sun, darkening the day, and filling the land with smoke.

On Wednesday morning at a quarter past five came the earthquake. A minute later the flames were leaping upward. In a
30 dozen different quarters south of Market Street in the working-class ghetto and in the factories, fires started. There was no opposing the flames. There was no organization, no communication. All the
35 cunning adjustments of a twentieth-century city had been smashed by the earthquake. The streets were humped into ridges and depressions and piled with the debris of fallen walls. The steel rails were twisted into
40 perpendicular and horizontal angles. The telephone and telegraph systems were disrupted. And the great water mains had

burst. All the shrewd contrivances and safe-guards of man had been thrown out of gear by
45 thirty seconds' twitching of the earth's crust.

—Excerpted from *The Story of an Eye-Witness* by Jack London

31. What do the vivid images the author creates throughout the passage convey?

(1) depression
(2) financial loss
(3) death
(4) destruction
(5) shock

32. To what does the phrase "lurid tower" refer?

(1) the flames
(2) the city
(3) the smoke
(4) the buildings
(5) the sun

33. According to the passage, how long did the earthquake itself last?

(1) 30 seconds
(2) a minute
(3) an hour
(4) an entire morning
(5) a day

34. Which of the following cannot be classified as a natural disaster?

(1) floods
(2) bombings
(3) tornadoes
(4) hurricanes
(5) droughts

35. The author focuses on damage to which of the following?

(1) people
(2) business
(3) transportation
(4) communication systems
(5) property

36. Later in his account, London talks about the tens of thousands who fled the earthquake. He says of them, "… yet everyone was gracious. The most perfect courtesy obtained."

According to this information, what did the author observe about the people's reaction to the damage of the earthquake?

(1) They acted as he had expected them to act.
(2) They hid their anger at losing their homes.
(3) They knew another quake was about to hit.
(4) They believed the destruction was not bad.
(5) They accepted nature's destruction with grace.

Questions 37–41 are based on the following passage.

WHAT CAN ATHLETES LEARN FROM DANCERS?

Lynn Swann, the great wide receiver of the Pittsburgh Steelers, started out as a dancer. His mother sent him to dancing school—jazz and tap—for fourteen years.
5 Yet by the sixth grade of elementary school in San Mateo, California, he was already a team member in the field of sports.

"Some of our greatest athletes might well have become some of our greatest
10 dancers if prejudice against dancing for men had not stood in the way," says Swann. "One can always see the presence of dance in sports. Both require endurance, agility, balance, strength and body controls of all
15 kinds. In sports the good athlete must know that if he needs to leap or jump, that the leap is for a specific purpose, that you are leaping at or leaping away from something. In ballet you learn that the landing from this
20 leap is the beginning of a move in a new direction. Athletes can use this."

Swann, who is on the board of directors of the Pittsburgh Ballet Theater, not only does TV commercials for this important
25 ballet company, but also practices ballet. Swann explains, "In Pittsburgh, and in any big city, we need culture as well as industry, art as well as sports. By my being on the ballet's board, I'm acting as a bridge
30 between the fans of our team and the fans of the ballet. And by doing this, I hope all of them will discover the similarities between two great activities."

—Excerpted from "How to Look at Dance"
by Walter Terry

37. What was Lynn Swann's profession?

(1) ballet dancer
(2) actor
(3) football player
(4) theater critic
(5) athletic coach

38. Which of the following is *not* mentioned in the passage as an attribute required in sports?

(1) endurance
(2) culture
(3) strength
(4) balance
(5) agility

39. Why does the author extensively quote Lynn Swann?

(1) to contrast the arts with business and industry
(2) to compare the author's viewpoint with Lynn Swann's
(3) to explain the similarities between dance and sports
(4) to encourage boys to participate in sports
(5) to persuade the reader to become a ballet fan

40. Which of the following athletic feats most closely resembles a ballet movement?

(1) a heavyweight champion knocking out his opponent in a prizefight
(2) a jockey heading toward the finish line in a horse race
(3) a shortstop fielding a grounder
(4) a basketball player leaping for a rebound
(5) a football player tackling the other team's quarterback

41. To what does the word *prejudice* in line 10 refer?

(1) discrimination against minorities in the performing arts
(2) Lynn Swann's intolerance of male dancers
(3) the biased image of athletes as "dumb jocks"
(4) discrimination against women in professional sports
(5) the attitudes stereotyping male dancers as unmasculine

Answers are on pages 97–99.

Business-Related Documents

Questions 42–46 are based on the following business-related document.

WHAT IS DIVERSITY IN THE WORKPLACE?

Recent research at Stanford Business School finds that diversity among employees can generate better performance when it comes to out-of-the-ordinary creative tasks.

Today's corporations are built around groups that must find answers to novel and complicated business issues. These teams bring together diverse groups of people who incorporate a variety of
5 backgrounds, ideas, or personalities. The Stanford Business School's Margaret Neale, the John G. McCoy-Banc One Corp. Professor of Organization and Dispute Resolution, and her colleagues have developed a rich body of research on diversity.

Diversity is … Well, Diverse

People tend to think of diversity as simply demographic, a matter of color, gender, or age. However,
10 groups can be disparate in many ways. Diversity is also based on informational differences, reflecting a person's education and experience, as well as on values or goals that can influence what one perceives to be the mission of something as small as a single meeting or as large as a whole company.

Diversity among employees can create better performance when it comes to out-of-the ordinary creative tasks such as product development or cracking new markets, and managers have
15 been trying to increase diversity to achieve the benefits of innovation and fresh ideas.

—Excerpted from the content library of *HRnext.com*

42. Which of the following situations would benefit most from diversity?

(1) responding to a customer's questions
(2) researching a product's effectiveness
(3) inventing a new consumer product
(4) mass-producing a household tool
(5) keeping current clients satisfied

43. What strategy, based on diversity, do companies use to solve workplace problems?

(1) hire outside consultants
(2) ask the executives
(3) survey customers
(4) train inexperienced workers
(5) use employee groups

44. According to the passage, which choice best defines *diversity*?

Companies with
(1) employees who have similar educational backgrounds
(2) employees from different countries and religions
(3) employees of different genders, races, and communities
(4) employees from different demographics, learning, and experience
(5) employees who have a long work experience with the company

45. What does the article suggest about modern business problems?

(1) They can destroy successful companies.
(2) They require innovative solutions.
(3) They result from changes in society.
(4) They damage a company's morale.
(5) They may need government action.

46. A communications company wants to plan for the next line of advances in communication technology in order to keep its customers supplied with the latest and most efficient devices.

According to this passage, how would this company best approach its goal?

(1) by consulting with business-school professionals
(2) by consulting a cross-section of its employees
(3) by studying the steps that the competition is taking
(4) by withholding information from their customers
(5) by asking various experts to devise a strategy

Questions 47–50 are based on the following form.

Family and Medical Leave Request Form

Employee: _____ Date: _____

Job Title: _____ Supervisor: _____

SSN #: _____

Eligible employees are entitled under the Family and Medical Leave Act (FMLA) to up to 12 weeks of job-protected leave for certain family and medical reasons. Submit this request form to your supervisor at least 30 days before the leave is to commence, when practicable. When submission of the request 30 days in advance is not practicable, submit the request as early as is practicable. The employer reserves the right to deny or postpone leave for failure to give appropriate notice when such denial/postponement would be permitted under federal or state law.

Eligibility

1. Counting any periods of time that you worked for the company (whether they were consecutive or not) have you worked for the company for a total of 12 months or more?

_____Yes _____No (If "yes," continue to the next question. If "no," stop here.)

2. During the past 12 months, have you worked at least 1,250 hours? (approximately eight months of 40-hour weeks or one year of 25-hour weeks)?

_____Yes _____No (If "yes," continue to the next question. If "no," stop here.)

3. Have you previously received medical or family leave? If yes, provide information below:

Dates of leave: From _____ To _____

Purpose of leave: _____

4. Have you taken any intermittent leave?

_____Yes _____No

5. Have you taken off from scheduled hours?

If "yes," provide details _____
_____

I am requesting leave for the following reason:

_____Personal serious health condition

_____Serious health condition of:

　　　Spouse's Name: _____

　　　Child's Name: _____

　　　Parent's Name: _____

_____Birth of a child: Expected delivery date is _____

_____Adoption of a child:

　　　Scheduled date of adoption_____

I am requesting leave from _____ to _____.

The total number of days of leave that I request is _____.

I agree to return to work on _____. If circumstances change as such I will not be able to return to work on that date, I agree to notify my supervisor by submitting NOTICE TO EMPLOYER OF CHANGES IN APPROVED MEDICAL OR FAMILY LEAVE form. I understand that my benefits will continue during my leave and that I will arrange to pay my share of applicable premiums.

Signature _____ Date _____

—Excerpted from "Family and Medical Leave Request Form" from the content library of *HRnext.com*

47. Based on this form, what is the purpose of the Family and Medical Leave Act?

    (1) to ensure that all workers have decent medical coverage

    (2) to guarantee job security while dealing with family emergencies

    (3) to protect employers from abuse of leave policies

    (4) to help families meet the stress of a financial ordeal

    (5) to identify employers who use unfair leave practices

48. When should an employee file the form requesting Family and Medical leave?

    (1) 30 days before the leave is needed

    (2) 12 weeks before the leave is needed

    (3) one week after beginning the leave

    (4) up to a year after the end of the leave

    (5) immediately upon learning of the need

49. What determines an employee's eligibility for obtaining leave?

    (1) seriousness of the illness

    (2) insurance coverage

    (3) supervisor's approval

    (4) length of time employed

    (5) number of family members

50. What must the employee agree to before the leave will be granted?

    (1) paying the company's share of the benefit cost

    (2) returning to work on a specified date

    (3) notifying the supervisor in writing on return

    (4) receiving a doctor's approval before returning

    (5) meeting with the supervisor each week of leave

Questions 51–54 are based on the following passage.

WHAT HAPPENS WHEN AN EMPLOYEE MISSES WORK FOR JURY DUTY?

The rules for paying employees while on jury duty are different for exempt and nonexempt employees. Under the federal Fair Labor Standards Act (FLSA), exempt employees who are absent from work to perform jury service must be paid their full salaries (exempts are those not covered by the FLSA's minimum wage and overtime requirements). However, the employer may deduct from
5 the salary any jury duty fees that the employee receives from the court. The FLSA does not require payment when the exempt employee is absent for one or more full weeks during which no work is performed.

The FSLA does not require employers to pay nonexempt salaried or hourly employees while on leave for jury duty.

10 A handful of state laws require employers to pay employees while on jury duty.

General pay practices. Although not required to do so, most employers do pay all employees, regardless of FLSA status, while on jury duty. According to BLR (Bureau of Labor Relations)'s 1997 Survey of Employee Benefits, more than 90 percent of employers nationwide offer paid leave for jury duty. The federal courts pay jurors a small fee, and many employers pay on the difference
15 between the jury duty pay and the employee's basic wage or salary. When paying the difference, it may be easiest to continue the employee's regular paychecks and have the employee endorse the jury duty checks over to the company.

Excuse from jury duty. An employee's loss of earnings is an unacceptable reason for being excused from jury duty. However, most courts will consider a request from an employer to
20 postpone jury service if the employee's absence would seriously interrupt company operations. This is only a temporary delay; eventually the employee will have to serve. Top management usually decides whether the company should ask the court to excuse an employee from jury duty. Address a request for postponement to the clerk of the appropriate court system as indicated on the jury summons.

25 **Job protection.** The federal Jury System Improvement Act of 1978 (28 USC Sec. 1875) prohibits employers from discharging permanent employees because they perform jury duty in federal court. Employers who violate the Act may be sued for back pay, reinstatement, and attorney's fees and may be fined up to $1,000.

—Excerpted from "Jury Duty" in the content library of *HRnext.com*

51. What is ensured by the Jury System Improvement Act of 1978?

(1) permanent exemption from jury duty for legitimate reasons
(2) the right of employees to keep all jury duty pay from federal courts
(3) prohibition from being released from a permanent position for jury duty
(4) the guarantee of minimum wage while on jury duty
(5) a fine of $1,000 for denying an employee jury duty pay

52. What should employees on jury duty do to determine if their employer must pay their salaries?

(1) find out if the state law requires employers to pay
(2) file a lawsuit in the federal courts for back pay
(3) ask the judge at the beginning of the trial
(4) request a postponement of their jury duty
(5) endorse their jury duty checks to their employers

53. Which type of employee is guaranteed to receive pay while on jury duty?

(1) temporary workers who hold no permanent job status
(2) employees who are exempt salaried personnel
(3) hourly employees who hold nonexempt job status
(4) exempt employees who serve jury duty for one full week
(5) employees covered by FLSA overtime requirements

54. What does the passage suggest by referring to BLR's 1997 Survey of Employee Benefits?

(1) that all employees nationwide do receive jury duty pay
(2) that jury duty pay is equivalent to the federal minimum wage
(3) that employers are entitled to a percentage of an employee's jury pay
(4) that the majority of employers pay employees for jury duty
(5) that federal courts pay jurors more than state courts do

Answers are on pages 99–100.

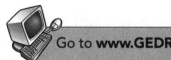

Go to **www.GEDReading.com** for additional practice and instruction!

Literary Nonfiction

The following passages are examples of literary nonfiction. Literary Nonfiction passages can be drawn from biographies, diaries, memoirs, letters, and essays.

Questions 1–7 are based on the following passage.

WHAT DO YOU LEARN ABOUT THE ASTRONAUT CHUCK YEAGER?

Yeager had started out as the equivalent, in the Second World War, of the legendary Frank Luke of the 27th Aero Squadron in the First. Which is to say, he
5 was the boondocker, the boy from the back country, with only a high school education, no credentials, no cachet or polish of any sort, who took off the feed-store overalls and put on a uniform and climbed into an
10 airplane and lit up the skies over Europe.

Yeager grew up in Hamlin, West Virginia, a town on the Mud River not far from Nitro, Hurricane Whirlwind, Salt Rock, Mud, Sod, Crum, Leet Dollie, Ruth, and Alum Creek.
15 His father was a gas driller (drilling for natural gas in the coalfields), his older brother was a gas driller, and he would have been a gas driller had he not enlisted in the Army Air Force in 1941 at the age of
20 eighteen. In 1943, at twenty, he became a flight officer, i.e. a non-com who was allowed to fly, and went to England to fly fighter planes over France and Germany. Even in the tumult of war Yeager was
25 somewhat puzzling to a lot of other pilots. He was a short, wiry, but muscular little guy with dark curly hair and tough-looking face that seemed (to strangers) to be saying: "You best not be lookin' at me in the eye, you
30 peckerwood, or I'll put four more holes in your nose." But that wasn't what was puzzling. What was puzzling was the way Yeager talked.

—Excerpted from *The Right Stuff* by Tom Wolfe

1. To whom can you conclude the word *boondocker* (line 5) refers?

   (1) a high school graduate
   (2) a World War II veteran
   (3) a European immigrant
   (4) a rural person
   (5) a squadron commander

2. What was the name of Yeager's hometown?

   (1) Nitro
   (2) Mud River
   (3) Salt Rock
   (4) Alum Creek
   (5) Hamlin

3. What did pilots find puzzling about Yeager?

   (1) his speech
   (2) his face
   (3) his physical threats
   (4) his manners
   (5) his heritage

4. What is the main purpose of the passage?

   (1) to analyze Yeager's professional conduct
   (2) to depict Yeager's character and background
   (3) to praise Yeager's heroic performance
   (4) to criticize Yeager's poor credentials
   (5) to discuss Yeager's military responsibilities

5. Why does the author include the following descriptive detail, "[Yeager] took off the feed-store overalls and put on a uniform" (lines 8–9)?

   (1) to suggest that Yeager was unexpectedly drafted
   (2) to illustrate an ex-farmhand's appearance
   (3) to vividly describe Yeager's change from a civilian to a pilot
   (4) to imply that people suddenly switch careers
   (5) to suggest that anyone can learn to fly

6. Which of the following qualities would the author probably consider most important to becoming a successful army pilot?

   (1) sophistication
   (2) wealth
   (3) formal education
   (4) communication skills
   (5) courage

7. In Tom Wolfe's book, *The Right Stuff*, the author describes the selection, training, and rocketing into space of the seven Mercury astronauts in the 1960s.

   Based on this information and the passage, why do you think Wolfe included Yeager in his book?

   (1) to demonstrate how pilots had improved
   (2) to show wartime and peacetime pilots
   (3) to introduce a pioneer with "the right stuff"
   (4) to point out the improvements in airplanes
   (5) to establish the need to educate astronauts

Questions 8–13 are based on the following passage.

WHAT DID JOE LOUIS ACCOMPLISH?

"He's off the ropes, ladies and gentlemen. He's moving towards the center of the ring." There was no time to be relieved. The worst might still happen.

5 "And now it looks like Joe is mad. He's caught Carnera with a left hook to the head and right to the head. It's a left jab to the body and another left to the head. There's a left cross and a right to the head. The
10 contender's right eye is bleeding and he can't seem to keep his block up. Louis is penetrating every block. The referee is moving in, but Louis sends a left to the body and it's an uppercut to the chin and the
15 contender is dropping … He's on the canvas, ladies and gentlemen."

Babies slid to the floor as women stood up and men leaned toward the radio.

"Here's the referee. He's counting. One,
20 two, three, four, five, six, seven … Is the contender trying to get up again?"

All the men in the store shouted, "NO!"

"—eight, nine, ten." There were a few sounds from the audience, but they seemed
25 to be holding themselves in against tremendous pressure.

"The fight is all over, ladies and gentlemen. Let's get the microphone over to the referee … Here he is. He's got the Brown Bomber's hand,
30 he's holding it up … Here he is … "

Then the voice, husky and familiar, came to wash over us—"The winnah, and still heavy-weight champeen of the world … Joe Louis."

Champion of the world. A Black boy.
35 Some Black mother's son. He was the strongest man in the world. People drank Coca-Colas like ambrosia and ate candy bars like Christmas. Some of the men went behind the store and poured white lightning in their
40 soft-drink bottles, and a few of the bigger boys followed them. Those who were not chased away came back blowing their breath in front of themselves like proud smokers.

—Excerpted from *I Know Why the Caged Bird Sings*
by Maya Angelou

8. Why did the author include the sports announcer's broadcast of the fight?

(1) to illustrate techniques of reporting sports events
(2) to comment on racial discrimination in professional sports
(3) to present a first-hand account of the action
(4) to contrast the sports announcer's viewpoint with the spectators'
(5) to reveal the sports announcer's tone of voice

9. Where have the people gathered to listen to the fight?

(1) a store
(2) a bar
(3) a restaurant
(4) an apartment
(5) an auditorium

10. According to paragraph 1, how does the author feel about the fight's outcome?

(1) confident
(2) terrified
(3) hopeless
(4) anxious
(5) relieved

11. What is the author's major purpose in the passage?

(1) to provide a blow-by-blow description of a heavyweight boxing match
(2) to show why people find boxing matches exciting
(3) to reveal the senseless violence of professional boxing
(4) to describe the festive mood following Joe Louis's victory
(5) to present Joe Louis as a heroic figure in black history

12. Which of the following artists would most
effectively portray a prizefighter's action?

   (1) a photographer
   (2) a cartoonist
   (3) a sculptor
   (4) a filmmaker
   (5) a painter

13. For the people listening to the fight in the
passage, Joe Louis was more than a boxing
champion: He was a proud symbol for their
race.

Why do you think the people were "holding
themselves in against tremendous pressure"
(lines 25–26)?

They were
   (1) trying not to get their hopes up too
       soon
   (2) afraid of the shame they would feel if he
       lost
   (3) anxious to cash in their winning bets on
       the fight
   (4) worried the owner would find them with
       the radio
   (5) ashamed that they were not doing their
       jobs

Questions 14–19 are based on the following passage.

WHAT DOES THE AUTHOR REMEMBER ABOUT HIS CHILDHOOD?

Down the forest-slopes to the left were the swings. They were made of bark stripped from hickory saplings. When they became dry they were dangerous. They
5 usually broke when a child was forty feet in the air, and this was why so many bones had to be mended every year. I had no ill luck myself, but none of my cousins escaped. There were eight of them and at one time
10 and another they broke fourteen arms among them. But it cost next to nothing, for the doctor worked by the year—twenty-five dollars for the whole family. I remember two of the Florida doctors, Chowning and
15 Meredith. They not only tended an entire family for twenty-five dollars a year but furnished the medicines themselves. Good measure, too. Only the largest persons could hold a whole dose. Castor oil was the
20 principal beverage. The dose was a half a dipperful, with a half a dipperful of New Orleans molasses added to help it down and make it taste good, which it never did. The next standby was calomel, the next rhubarb,
25 and the next jalap. Then they bled the patient and put mustard plasters on him. It was a dreadful system and yet the death-rate was not heavy. The calomel was nearly sure to salivate the patient and cost him
30 some of his teeth. There were no dentists. When teeth became touched with decay or were otherwise ailing, the doctor knew of but one thing to do: he fetched his tongs and dragged them out. If the jaw remained,
35 it was not his fault. Doctors were not called in cases of ordinary illnesses; the family grandmother attended to those. Every old woman was a doctor and gathered her own medicines in the woods, and knew how to
40 compound doses that would stir the vitals of a cast-iron dog.

—Excerpted from *Memories of a Missouri Farm* by Mark Twain

14. What is the main topic of the passage?

(1) children's injuries
(2) medical practices
(3) family relationships
(4) homemade drugs
(5) cheap medical bills

15. Why does the author begin the paragraph with a description of the swings and the accidents they cause?

(1) to describe a frightening childhood memory
(2) to imply the conflict between the author and his cousins
(3) to establish the joyous atmosphere of the setting
(4) to criticize children for playing with hazardous toy
(5) to introduce an example of injuries requiring medical attention

16. Who treated ordinary illnesses?

(1) Dr. Chowning
(2) Dr. Meredith
(3) the family grandmother
(4) the author's cousins
(5) the dentist

17. According to the passage, what happened when someone had a toothache or a cavity?

(1) A doctor pulled out the tooth with tongs.
(2) A dentist put a filling in the decayed tooth.
(3) A doctor operated on the patient's jaw.
(4) The patient swallowed large doses of castor oil.
(5) The patient salivated and lost his or her teeth.

18. How would a modern physician most likely consider Dr. Chowning and Dr. Meredith's treatments?

(1) sophisticated
(2) dangerous
(3) innovative
(4) practical
(5) silly

19. The author of Mark Twain's biography commented that Twain's experiences on the farm were a valuable and lasting education that influenced his writing.

Based on this information and the passage, what can you infer that Twain learned from his life on the farm that can be found in his writing style?

(1) Doctors really don't know much.
(2) People need to look at life with humor.
(3) Farmers suffer from many illnesses.
(4) Grandmothers' remedies are harmful.
(5) Childhood had many good moments.

Questions 20–25 are based on the following passage.

WHAT ARE THE AUTHOR'S MEMORIES OF TED JOHNSON?

I look up from this saga on my place mat to recall, in the midst of travel, the tiny oasis of my youth, Ted Johnson's Standard. On our block flew the Texaco star and the Mobil
(5) horse, but you couldn't pay us not to fill our Pontiac at Ted Johnson's Standard. He was the magician of the fan belt. With an old rag and one tough weathered hand, he took on radiators foaming and in flame. Where other
(10) men displayed girly calendars, Ted Johnson hung the green cross of safety.

Although he looked like Smokey the Bear, it was engine neglect and rowdy driving that he cautioned against. Whenever
(15) a kid short-cut onto Bridge Street across his pumps, old Ted raised the finger of warning. "Stay to the right, sonny," he would yell, shaking his gray head over the lapse in safety. He had spotless pumps, his rest
(20) rooms glowed in the dark, he bleached the windshield sponges, but it was safety that drew us all to Ted. He wouldn't take your money until he had checked your spare. And it must have worked. He never lost a regular
(25) customer to a traffic fatality. He kept the number of deathless days posted above his cash register. At night, after he counted his receipts, Ted read the obituaries and added another safety day. I remember at least
(30) 7,300. Twenty years of Ted's customers rolling down the road with their spare tires at the ready. They didn't need their suction-cup saints. Ted passed out his own stick-on mottoes for the dashboard.

(35) DON'T SWITCH LANES
ALWAYS SIGNAL FIRST
USE THE REARVIEW MIRROR
—Excerpted from "Gas Stations" by Max Apple

20. According to the author, what most attracted customers to Ted's station?

(1) his spotless gas pumps
(2) his concern for safety
(3) his bleached windshield sponges
(4) his glowing rest rooms
(5) his skill as an auto mechanic

21. Why does the author refer to Ted as the "magician of the fan belt" (line 7)?

(1) Ted performed magic tricks at the gas station.
(2) Ted's personality enchanted all of his customers.
(3) Ted fanned a flaming radiator with one hand.
(4) Ted's ability to repair engines was amazing.
(5) Ted made fan belt problems miraculously disappear.

22. What would Ted probably say to a drunken driver who pulled into his gas station?

(1) "Avoid heavy traffic on the expressway!"
(2) "Drive your car slowly and cautiously!"
(3) "Don't drive your car until you're sober!"
(4) "Don't fall asleep at the wheel!"
(5) "You are a menace to society!"

23. Which of the following steps did Ted *not* take to promote sound driving habits?

(1) scolding rowdy drivers
(2) passing out stick-on mottoes
(3) checking spare tires
(4) registering the causes of traffic fatalities
(5) posting the number of deathless days

24. Which word or phrase best describes Ted's behavior?

(1) money-conscious
(2) caring
(3) morbid
(4) short-tempered
(5) meddling

25. In what other literary form would the techniques that the author uses in portraying Ted's character also be effective?

(1) a short story
(2) a poem
(3) a newspaper obituary
(4) a play
(5) a case study

Questions 26–30 are based on the following passage.

WHAT KIND OF CHARACTERS ARE FOLK HEROES?

Folk heroes are usually supermen. The heroes of the American frontier were super-strong, unflinchingly brave, and unusually keen—just as we would secretly like to be.
5 Many of these heroes, like Davy Crockett, lived and helped create some of the yarns. Some of them, like Paul Bunyan, were pure invention and inspiration. In any event, all these heroes are interesting to us. They tell
10 us much about our American past and display a typically American brand of humor—that of deliberate exaggeration, or the tall tale.

Some of the tall tales make familiar
15 reading. Many a present-day radio or television comedian has gone back to these picturesque liars for inspiration. No one knows how old some of the stories are. The tall tales usually run something like this. A
20 man is pursued by a mountain lion. At the last moment, just as the lion opens his mouth to take a bite, the man turns and reaches down the lion's throat. He grabs the tail and pulls the lion inside out. The lion
25 then keeps running in the opposite direction, and the man is saved.

—Excerpted from *Myths and Folklore* by Henry I. Christ

26. How can the overall tone of the passage best be described?

    (1) comical
    (2) impersonal
    (3) inspirational
    (4) critical
    (5) informative

27. What assumption does the author make about the reader?

    That the reader
    (1) studies American history
    (2) admires heroic behavior
    (3) analyzes styles of humor
    (4) reveals confidential secrets
    (5) avoids telling lies

28. Which of the following women best represents a modern-day folk hero?

    (1) Whoopi Goldberg, a popular movie and TV comedienne
    (2) Toni Morrison, winner of the Nobel Prize for literature
    (3) Sally Ride, the first female astronaut
    (4) Hillary Rodham Clinton, former First Lady and U.S. Senator
    (5) Barbara Walters, popular TV news personality

29. According to the passage, which of the following storytelling devices distinguishes tall tales from other types of fiction?

    (1) interesting heroes
    (2) historical settings
    (3) imaginary situations
    (4) deliberate exaggeration
    (5) familiar characters

30. What is the main purpose of the second paragraph?

    (1) to analyze the vicious behavior of mountain lions
    (2) to illustrate the plot of a tall tale
    (3) to suggest that TV comedy routines are dishonest
    (4) to pinpoint the historical origin of the tall tale
    (5) to explain why folktales are easy to read

Questions 31–36 are based on the following passage.

WHO WAS THE SPANISH POET FEDERICO GARCIA LORCA?

The Spanish poet Federico Garcia Lorca spent some time in New York and in Cuba when he was in his early thirties. In 1936, when he was thirty-eight, Lorca was killed by the
5 Fascists during the Spanish Civil War. His early poems, written in Andalusia, where he was born, are often like strange folk tales or fairy tales—sometimes stories about nature, some- times about the lives of the gypsies. The poems
10 written in New York are rougher and freer and less songlike and have other subjects.

Lorca's poetry is always wild and strange in one way or another. There are mysterious places and unexplainable things and
15 extraordinary events. There is a forest of stuffed doves, a salon with a thousand windows, a paper sea, a black water car. Money "sobs in the pocket," the New York dawn has "four columns of slime," the "palm
20 tree wants to be a stork." Lorca's way of writing makes everything he writes about seem mysterious and strange.

You are probably used to the way a place, for instance the town you live in,
25 looks completely different to you depending on your mood, your feelings. One day it is beautiful; another day it is horrible. What is inside you always changes what is outside you. In his poetry Lorca doesn't try to
30 separate what he is feeling from what is outside him. Instead, he seems to allow what he is feeling and thinking to transform what is around him.

—Excerpted from *Sleeping on the Wing*
by Kenneth Koch and Kate Farrell

31. Which of the following statements is *not* a fact?

　(1) Lorca was born in Andalusia, Spain.
　(2) Lorca died when he was thirty-eight years old.
　(3) Fascists killed Lorca during the Spanish Civil War.
　(4) Lorca's stay in New York changed his poetic style.
　(5) During his thirties, Lorca spent some time in Cuba.

32. How can the images quoted from Lorca's poetry best be described?

　(1) rough
　(2) songlike
　(3) strange
　(4) realistic
　(5) literal

33. In what way do the authors believe a depressed person views a sunny day?

　(1) cheerful
　(2) beautiful
　(3) gloomy
　(4) mysterious
　(5) unexplainable

34. What is the authors' major purpose in writing the passage?

　To show Lorca's
　(1) moodiness
　(2) imagination
　(3) political beliefs
　(4) travel experiences
　(5) Spanish heritage

35. What technique do the authors use to involve the reader?

　(1) using the pronoun *you* in the third paragraph
　(2) reporting biographical information in the first paragraph
　(3) revealing their personal impressions of Lorca's poetry
　(4) interpreting the meaning of Lorca's figurative language
　(5) explaining that Lorca also wrote poetry in America

36. Until 40 years after Lorca's death in 1936, the Spanish government, whose troops killed him, prohibited his books and forbade the mention of his name.

Based on this information and the passage, what was the most likely effect of banning Lorca's name and his works?

　(1) It angered the men who killed him.
　(2) It made Lorca unpopular with the public.
　(3) It forced an investigation of his death.
　(4) It gave him heroic stature with the people.
　(5) It questioned his lack of literary talent.

Questions 37–41 are based on the following passage.

WHAT DOES THE BOOK REVIEW SAY ABOUT *DREAMGIRL: MY LIFE AS A SUPREME?*

Diana Ross was a scene-stealing, manipulative, ambitious prima donna, says former Supreme Mary Wilson in her new book, *Dreamgirl: My Life As a Supreme* (St.
5 Martin's Press). The original Supremes, who went on to become the most commercially successful female singing group of the 1960s, had three lead singers (Ross, Wilson, and the late Florence Ballard), but almost from the
10 start Ross set out to take center stage.

"Diane"—as Wilson pointedly calls her throughout the book, recalling her own amusement when Ross announced in an interview that "Diana" was her "real" name—
15 would often arrive at public appearances at the last minute, calling attention to herself by showing up in a dress different from the one the three women had agreed to wear. According to Wilson, Ross threw temper
20 tantrums and fought with other Motown Records' artists; changed the name of the group to "Diana Ross and the Supremes" (supported by mentor-lover, Motown chief Berry Gordy); eased Ballard out; and actually
25 pushed Wilson away from the microphone when they were performing at Motown's anniversary special in 1983.

None of this comes as a shock. It is, however, the first legitimate confirmation of the
30 rumors that have surrounded the Supremes' legend for years. And Wilson's book is much more than an exposé. She manages to avoid making Ross the real star of the story by providing a wealth of information about the
35 early days at Motown. One reads about the cramped recording studio in the "Hitsville" building at 2648 Grand Boulevard in Detroit as well as about the love and camaraderie among such musicians as Marvin Gaye, Smokey Rob-
40 inson and The Miracles, The Temptations, The Four Tops, Martha Reeves and The Vandellas, The Marvelettes, Mary Wells, and Jr. Walker— many of whom started out together as kids, and wound up making some of the most impor-
45 tant music of the 1960s.

—Excerpted from *Supreme Insult* by Lisa Robinson

37. Why is the introductory sentence effective in capturing the reader's attention?

 (1) It states the author, the title, and the publisher.
 (2) Mary Wilson's insulting remark is direct and hard hitting.
 (3) It arouses the interest of Diana Ross's most devoted fans.
 (4) It objectively summarizes Diana Ross's onstage personality.
 (5) It compares Diana Ross to other star performers.

38. Which word would the reviewer probably use to summarize Mary Wilson's book?

 (1) shocking
 (2) legendary
 (3) scandalous
 (4) informative
 (5) amusing

39. According to the passage, what caused the conflict between Diana Ross and Mary Wilson?

 (1) Mary Wilson's jealousy
 (2) Diana Ross's behavior
 (3) Florence Ballard's death
 (4) Berry Gordy's decisions
 (5) the Supremes' popularity

40. What does the reviewer find especially noteworthy about Mary Wilson's book?

 (1) the accounts of Diana Ross's temper tantrums and fights
 (2) the star role that Diana Ross plays in the story
 (3) the bitter competition among the Motown groups
 (4) the one-sided characterization of Diana Ross
 (5) the wealth of facts and details about Motown's early days

41. Which of the following was *not* a Motown band in the 1960s?

 (1) Martha Reeves and The Vandellas
 (2) The Marvelettes
 (3) The Supremes
 (4) The Dreamgirls
 (5) The Temptations

Answers are on pages 100–102.

Visual Nonfiction

The following selections are examples of visual nonfiction. Visual Nonfiction passages are writings about film, photography, television, art, painting, and sculpture.

Questions 1–4 are based on the following passage.

WHY IS *FRANKENSTEIN* A BREATHTAKING HORROR MOVIE?

In many respects *Frankenstein* was a breathtaking motion picture, although it too suffered from the same artistic problems evident in *Dracula*. Starting from the opening
5 atmospheric shots in a tiny, isolated village graveyard, [director] Whale established a remarkable mood, and increased the effects by carrying the action over to the medieval castle and eventually reaching some of the
10 finest moments in all the terror films in the misguided scientist's secret laboratory. Whale, in excellently designed shots aided considerably by the distinguished camera work of the experienced Arthur Edeson and
15 the remarkable sets of art designer Herman Rosse, created a marvelous sequence in which Professor Waldman comes to watch his former student's supernatural experiment. At first the cautious scholar and
20 the expelled Frankenstein review the controversial nature of the tests being carried on with ultra-violet rays, dead animals and human transplants. Henry claims that he has gone further than any mortal has
25 yet dared venture, and triumphantly reveals his masterpiece. Dr. Waldman is horrified, and even more skeptical that such a thing can be given life. Then Frankenstein demonstrates how the synthetic man can be
30 created. In a series of thrilling camera angles, extremely well-paced and owing much to the laboratory scenes in *Metropolis*, the unorthodox experimenter mechanically raises the body of the monster to a
35 predetermined opening in the ceiling where flying kites attract the lightning bolts from the raging storm. There in the electrifying darkness of night, sparks, currents, dials, electrodes, and levers capture our eyes.

40 Finally the nameless creature is lowered back to the surgical table. Everyone's attention is riveted to the hideous, still bandaged form. The ugly hand of the monster begins to move, and Frankenstein,
45 delirious with joy, screams, "He's alive! He's alive I tell you! He's alive!"

—Excerpted from *Terrors of the Screen* by Frank Manchel

1. What word does the author use to describe the art designer's sets?

   (1) marvelous
   (2) excellent
   (3) misguided
   (4) remarkable
   (5) supernatural

2. Why is the last sentence effective?

   (1) It vividly describes one of the most dramatic moments in the movie.
   (2) It shows the screenwriter's skill in creating realistic dialogue.
   (3) It portrays the final scene in the movie when the monster is "born."
   (4) It summarizes the author's characterization of Frankenstein.
   (5) It suggests the importance of scientific discovery.

3. What is the author's central purpose?

   (1) to describe the creation of the monster
   (2) to compare two classic movies
   (3) to analyze the expert camera work
   (4) to describe Dr. Waldman's horror
   (5) to criticize the director of Dracula

4. Which of the following scientific advances would have most interested Dr. Frankenstein?

   (1) nuclear weapons
   (2) laser-beam surgery
   (3) cloning
   (4) kidney transplants
   (5) computerized medicine

Questions 5–8 are based on the following passage.

WHAT STORY DOES THE MOVIE *IT'S A WONDERFUL LIFE* TELL?

The movie's apparently simple plot hid reversals and twisted chronologies typical of postwar films. It began like a fairy tale, with Capra swinging upward from the opening
5   shots of buildings and their chorus of prayers to a luminous heaven where the voices of God and Chief Angel Joseph issued from pulsating stars. Summoning a smaller star (Angel Second Class Clarence
10 Oddbody, yet to earn his wings after 200 years), the voices explained that George Bailey was about to commit suicide. Clarence (Henry Travers) would have one hour to learn about George before
15 descending to Earth to help him. What followed was a long, film noir-like flashback, covering George's life up to the present. (The film did not quite live up to its promised time limit; George's story required
20 not an hour, but nearly 100 minutes.)

George, it appeared, was a good man, married with four children. He had dreamed of great things but ended up spending his entire life in Bedford Falls, managing the
25 Bailey Building and Loan, which lent money to small homeowners too poor to get credit from the bank, owned (like everything else in town) by Mr. Potter (Lionel Barrymore). On Christmas Eve, George's Uncle Billy
30 (Thomas Mitchell), a warm-hearted, but slightly addled man, absentmindedly misplaced $8,000 intended for deposit. Inevitably, the money fell into Potter's hands. With the bank examiner paying an
35 unexpected visit, and without the funds to balance the books, George faced ruin. With no solutions in sight, he decided to drown himself to leave his family with the proceeds from his meager life insurance policy. Just as
40 he was about to jump off a bridge, however, Clarence materialized, jumped in first, and called for help. George instinctively jumped in to save him but refused to accept Clarence's subsequent explanation: "I'm
45 your guardian angel. I've come here to help you." Unable to rid George of his despair,

Clarence determined to answer his wish: "I wish I had never been born." The ensuing sequence took George on a tour of Bedford
50 Falls (now "Pottersville") to show him the "results" of his never having lived. Terrified by this vision, George prayed to be allowed to live again. The wish granted, he returned home to find that his wife and friends had
55 raised the money to meet the bank shortfall and to learn that he had, after all, lived a wonderful life.

Summarized in this way, *It's a Wonderful Life* would appear mawkishly sentimental. In
60 fact, it was almost frighteningly bleak for most of its 129 minutes.

—Excerpted from *A Certain Tendency of the Hollywood Cinema 1930–1980* by Robert B. Ray

5. What is the author's purpose for the arrangement of the supporting details in the passage?

(1) to compare the plot to typical Hollywood films
(2) to analyze the film's Christmas message
(3) to judge the actors' abilities
(4) to trace the sequence of events
(5) to explain the director's film techniques

6. Which of the following choices is an opinion?

(1) The film uses flashback techniques to tell George's story.
(2) The film is approximately 129 minutes long.
(3) The opening scene is like a fairy tale.
(4) The film was made after World War II.
(5) Lionel Barrymore plays the role of a wealthy man.

7. Why was a guardian angel trying to help George Bailey?

(1) George was on the verge of bankruptcy.
(2) George was about to commit suicide.
(3) George's family was in despair.
(4) George was terrified of his past.
(5) George's insurance policy expired.

8. Which of the following movies has a plot similar to that of *It's a Wonderful Life?*

(1) *A Christmas Carol,* in which three ghosts show the main character the joy of Christmas and of life

(2) *Braveheart,* in which a Scottish hero fights for freedom

(3) *Titanic,* in which a large luxury liner strikes an iceberg and sinks

(4) *Jaws,* in which a shark terrorizes a resort town

(5) *Jurassic Park,* in which dinosaurs go on a rampage

Questions 9–13 are based on the following passage.

WHAT SUBJECT FASCINATES THE PLAYWRIGHT JOHN LOGAN?

"Whenever I write about Leopold and Loeb," says playwright John Logan, "I feel their ghosts hovering over me and, oddly enough, a sense of responsibility. I feel
5 compelled to promise not to mess up their story, to tell it honestly and effectively."

Logan was speaking of Nathan Leopold, Jr. and Richard Loeb, the Chicago youths who, in 1924, kidnapped little Bobby Franks,
10 bludgeoned him to death and thus became two of the most notorious figures in the history of crime.

But Logan could well have been delivering his own artistic credo. Of all the
15 young playwrights scribbling in the off-Loop arena, Logan seems to have the most singular mission. He writes about sensational murders, the ones that make tabloid headlines in their time and fascinate
20 criminologists forever afterward.

A lot of docu-dramatists and made-for-television movie scenarists do that. But Logan has a unique ability to climb inside the minds of his killers (or accused killers)
25 and present their motives and feelings, as well as chronicled facts. In "Never the Sinner," which Stormfield Theatre produced in 1985 and which has been optioned for a London production, Logan detailed
30 convincing glimpses of what he imagines the emotional relationship between Leopold and Loeb might have been like. (In fact, there is almost no record of what they said privately to one another.)

—Excerpted from "Crime Does Pay" by Sid Smith

9. Who were Leopold and Loeb?

  (1) fictional characters
  (2) murderers
  (3) actors
  (4) kidnap victims
  (5) playwrights

10. Why is Logan's statement, "I feel their ghosts hovering over me" (lines 2–3) effective?

  (1) It reveals his haunting and ghoulish personality.
  (2) It explains the spooky atmosphere of his plays.
  (3) It describes his decision to write about the supernatural.
  (4) It suggests that he feels the actual presence of characters.
  (5) It proves that he is psychic and communicates with the dead.

11. Which of the following headlines would probably interest Logan?

  (1) Cops Shoot Burglar in Self-Defense
  (2) Lizzie Borden Kills Her Parents with an Ax
  (3) Two Drunken Fans Brawl After the Super Bowl
  (4) Two Teenagers Kill Themselves in a Suicide Pact
  (5) Youth Accidentally Sets Garage on Fire

12. According to the reviewer, what is Logan's unique ability?

  (1) He tells stories honestly and effectively.
  (2) He understands the psychological makeup of crime victims.
  (3) He distorts newspaper accounts of crimes.
  (4) He frightens audiences with gory details.
  (5) He delves into the emotions and motives of the criminal mind.

13. What can the reader infer that Logan does before he writes a script?

  (1) He watches documentaries.
  (2) He travels to other countries.
  (3) He analyzes children's stories.
  (4) He conducts library research.
  (5) He reviews made-for-TV movies.

Questions 14–18 are based on the following passage.

WHY DO PERFORMING ARTISTS EXPERIENCE STAGEFRIGHT?

It is an impartial disease, striking both the great and the small. The symptoms vary but are always unpleasant: nausea, pounding heart, weak knees, chattering
5   teeth, and, in severe cases, thickened speech, memory failure, and even blindness.

Carol Channing, a victim, was repulsed by all foods and couldn't eat for three days before the opening of *Hello, Dolly!* Helen
10 Hayes once went deaf from it and couldn't even hear her applause. The disease, of course, is stagefright, and, while we, the audience, never give it a thought, to performers it can mean lifelong suffering.
15 "Any actor who claims he's not frightened," Lynn Fontaine once insisted, "just isn't telling the truth."

Although the U.S. Office of Education has sponsored research into its causes and
20 cures, stagefright remains a common occupational hazard endemic to all theatrical occupations. Katharine Cornell was nervous every night of her career, and only managed to control it by "repetition of the feeling
25 that you can't be sick on stage." Violinist Kato Havas wrote a book on it, devoting whole chapters to such subjects as "The Fear of Dropping the Violin."

The causes are varied and can be as
30 specific as last-minute changes or a noisy audience. Usually, however, it is Ego that takes the blame. Performers, like the rest of us, want to be admired for their work. And they also feel a tremendous responsibility to
35 their fellow performers, and to their audience.

—Excerpted from "Stagefright!" by Alan M. Brown

14. What method of organization does the author use in the first paragraph to introduce the topic?

(1) analysis of causes
(2) explanation of a process
(3) comparison and contrast
(4) examples of effects
(5) classification of information

15. Which of the following people wrote a book about stagefright?

(1) Lynn Fontaine
(2) Kato Havas
(3) Helen Hayes
(4) Katharine Cornell
(5) Carol Channing

16. In which of the following situations would the average person probably experience a form of stagefright?

(1) watching a horror movie
(2) moving into a new apartment
(3) witnessing a bank robbery
(4) going to the dentist
(5) interviewing for an important job

17. According to the author, what causes performers to experience stagefright?

(1) fear of bad reviews and unemployment
(2) failure to memorize the script
(3) responsibility for impressing the audience
(4) negative opinions of noisy audiences
(5) resentment of other actors

18. Which of the following inferences about stagefright is valid?

(1) Only famous actors suffer continuously from stagefright.
(2) People afflicted with stagefright usually become deaf.
(3) The symptoms of stagefright are both physical and psychological.
(4) The U.S. Office of Education has discovered the cure for stagefright.
(5) Theater audiences sympathize with actors' performance pressures.

Questions 19–23 are based on the following passage.

WHAT IS THE ARCHITECTURAL DESIGN OF SOME MODERN HOSPITALS?

At first glance, the emergency center at Baptist Hospital in Miami seems fit for a king, not a patient. Shaded by an enormous oak tree, the lobby soars upward to a
5 skylight set in a vaulted ceiling. The floor is gleaming charcoal tile, the registration desk rose and buff toned, the walls soft gray. Postmodern clichés abound: a pair of coral classical columns, an ivory yellow cornice.
10 Pain and blood—the staples of most frantic emergency wards—are missing. There are no stark white rooms, no dark halls, no grim, impatient nurses.

For centuries, the word *hospital* sum-
15 moned up images of suffering and death. But as the Baptist Hospital emergency center—and scores of other new facilities around the country—proves, this tradition is changing fast. The 1980s revolution in health
20 care, spurred by new tools, attitudes and cures that prolong life, is matched by a similar revolution in architecture. Gone is the antiseptic, white-on-white look, replaced by a flood of fanciful arches, skylit atriums and
25 chic pastels.

Lavish decors: What's more, as health care has become a $400 billion dollar industry and privately owned chains like Humana enter a field once dominated by
30 churches, charities and local governments, the patient has become transformed from supplicant to highly valued consumer. Now he has his choice of exercise-intensive health parks; of small outpatient clinics, where
35 simple surgery can be performed at low cost; of specialized hospitals for women, for children and for the elderly that sport lavish decors.

—Excerpted from "The New High-Style Hospital" by
Douglas Davis with Nikki Finke Greenberg

19. What are the authors suggesting that the emergency center reminds them of in lines 1–3, "At first glance, the emergency center at Baptist Hospital in Miami seems fit for a king, not a patient"?

(1) a dungeon
(2) a castle
(3) a beach resort
(4) a torture chamber
(5) a church

20. According to the authors, what images does the word *hospital* historically bring to mind?

(1) pain and blood
(2) lavish decor
(3) dark, bleak halls
(4) suffering and death
(5) grim, impatient nurses

21. According to the authors, what factors helped to create the 1980s revolution in health care?

(1) advances in medical technology and changing attitudes
(2) donations from wealthy citizens
(3) new hospital furniture and better cafeteria food
(4) setbacks in medical research and cutbacks in funding
(5) an increase in people's life spans

22. Where would the authors probably recommend that a pregnant woman have her child delivered?

(1) in a small outpatient clinic
(2) in a specialized women's hospital
(3) in a frantic emergency ward
(4) in a Humana-owned hospital
(5) in a specialized children's hospital

23. For which magazine article subject would the author of this passage's style be appropriate?

(1) medical malpractice
(2) new surgical procedures
(3) health care for the elderly
(4) life-threatening illnesses
(5) doctors' waiting rooms

Questions 24–28 are based on the following passage.

WHAT DID HORACE PIPPIN, A BLACK WORLD WAR I VETERAN, PORTRAY IN HIS ART?

The burnt wood panel was the basis of one of his most famous paintings. It was something he had thought about for years—the coming of peace on the battlefield. He
5 called it *The End of the War: Starting Home.* He worked on it for three years. He piled one coat of paint on top of another until at last it was thick with paint, so much so that it appears almost carved. And instead of
10 making an ordinary picture frame, Pippin carved grenades, tanks, bombs, rifles, bayonets, and gas masks into a heavy frame.

In the painting, German soldiers are emerging from trenches and dugouts to
15 surrender to Black soldiers, amid a tangle of barbed wire in a great thicket of bare trees before a desolate mountain. In the sky, bombs burst and planes fall in flames. It is a hauntingly grim picture, the faces of all the
20 soldiers without expression. No one looks triumphant. The earth itself appears destroyed. This picture of utter destruction and desolation, so patiently and intensely worked over by a man wounded and
25 disabled in the war, is a profound antiwar painting. In it everything is destroyed. Even the end of the war is not a triumph for the victors.

In the next few years Pippin created four
30 more war paintings. In each one he showed the life of Black soldiers. The eloquence of these paintings does not lie in horrible scenes of slaughter, but in their direct, grim portrayal of the desolation of the world.

35 Because of his injured arm Pippin could not paint with spontaneous brush strokes. His work was preconceived and extraordinary in design and color.

—Excerpted from *Six Black Masters of American Art* by Romare Bearden and Harry Henderson

24. Which phrase best summarizes what Pippin depicts in *The End of the War: Starting Home?*

    (1) planes falling in flames
    (2) horrible images of slaughter
    (3) Germans surrendering to black soldiers
    (4) a desolate and profound antiwar scene
    (5) the destruction of the earth

25. Which of the following people would probably find Pippin's artistic abilities the most inspirational?

    (1) disabled veterans
    (2) modern painters
    (3) prisoners of war
    (4) German soldiers
    (5) art dealers

26. What artistic technique is used in *The End of the War: Starting Home?*

    (1) painting with spontaneous brush strokes
    (2) layering several coats of paint
    (3) carving scenes on the canvas
    (4) burning images into a panel
    (5) designing extraordinary colors

27. What kind of language does the author use in explaining Pippin's paintings?

    (1) figurative
    (2) technical
    (3) conversational
    (4) descriptive
    (5) formal

28. What does Pippin show in the war paintings mentioned in the passage?

    (1) the triumph of the victors
    (2) the lives of black soldiers
    (3) the heroic expressions on soldiers' faces
    (4) the brute strength of the Germans
    (5) the scenic landscape of the battlefield

Questions 29–33 are based on the following passage.

WHAT IS FOLK ART?

One of the wonderful things about folk art is it expresses an inner patience on the part of the artist, something that is uncommon when you walk through
5   contemporary galleries filled with abstract and minimalist images. Quilts, wood carvings and other things that are both useful and ornamental are the typical media of the folk artist, and the best of them
10 reflect a vision undistorted by the need to hurry through life.

The current exhibit in the lobby of the Shedd Aquarium, 1200 S. Lake Shore Dr., offers a chance to enjoy a slice of American
15 folk art at its best. Called "Wooden Waves, Quilted Seas: Aquatic Themes in American Folk Art," it comprises 40 pieces from the 19th and 20th Centuries belonging to local collectors and the Henry Ford Museum in
20 Michigan. One message of the show is that if most folk artists are patient souls, these pieces were made by people who were positively serene.

At least most of the time. Among the
25 exhibits of quilts, fence post ornaments, a weather vane, and even a carousel "sea horse," there is one particularly touching piece. It is scrimshaw, intricate etching on a piece of whalebone, that looks like a
30 valentine to a lover. It is obvious the artist, a sailor, had plenty of time to think about "Caroline," whose name is carved across the middle of the piece. Among the many images over its large surface is the principal one of
35 Caroline herself, in a full, bustled dress and with a pair of binoculars, gazing into the distance. This is obviously the way our lonely sailor preferred to imagine his woman, for whom he devoted so many hours.

—Excerpted from "Shedd Shows American Folk Art at Its Best" by Jay Pridmore

29. What is the author's main purpose in writing the passage?

(1) to compare folk art with contemporary paintings
(2) to teach methods used in crafting folk art
(3) to review the folk art exhibit at the Shedd Aquarium
(4) to show how folk art represents American culture
(5) to explain why local collectors value folk art

30. How does the author characterize folk artists?

(1) hurried
(2) uncommon
(3) touching
(4) patient
(5) undistorted

31. Which of the following objects would probably *not* be classified as folk art?

(1) an embroidered tablecloth
(2) a marble sculpture
(3) a 19th century Christmas ornament
(4) a handwoven rug
(5) a carved wooden chest

32. What can you infer that the word *aquatic* (line 16) means?

Something associated with
(1) crafts
(2) sailors
(3) fish
(4) museums
(5) water

33. What does the writer use an emotional tone to describe?

His impressions of a
(1) handmade quilt
(2) whalebone etching
(3) fence post ornament
(4) weather vane
(5) carousel sea horse

Answers are on pages 102–104.

Chapter 2

Prose Fiction

GED Language Arts, Reading pages 165–215
Complete GED pages 589–614

Prose Fiction includes excerpts from novels, short stories, and classical and popular tales.

The excerpts on pages 37–42 are from works written before 1920.

Questions 1–5 are based on the following passage.

WHAT IS DOROTHEA FEELING?

Dorothea was in the reaction of a rebellious anger stronger than any she had felt
since her marriage. Instead of tears there
came words:— "What have I done—what
5 am I—that he should treat me so? He never
knows what is in my mind—he never cares.
What is the use of anything I do? He wishes
he had never married me." She began to
hear herself, and was checked into stillness.
10 Like one who has lost his way and is weary,
she sat and saw as in one glance all the
paths of her young hope which she should
never find again. And just as clearly in the
miserable light she saw her own and her
15 husband's solitude—how they walked apart
so that she was obliged to survey him. If he
had drawn her towards him, she would
never have surveyed him—never have said,
"Is he worth living for?" but would have felt
20 him simply a part of her own life. Now she
said bitterly, "It is his fault, not mine." In the
jar of her whole being, pity was overthrown.
Was it her fault that she had believed in
him—had believed in his worthiness?—And
25 what, exactly, was he? ... In such a crisis as
this, some women begin to hate.

—Excerpted from *Middlemarch* by George Eliot

1. Which word best describes Dorothea's
   mood in this passage?

   (1) joyous
   (2) angry
   (3) fearful
   (4) sarcastic
   (5) loving

2. " ... she sat and saw as in one glance all the
   paths of her young hope which she should
   never find again" (lines 11–13). What does
   Dorothea realize in this moment?

   (1) that the path behind her house has been
       washed away
   (2) that she cannot communicate with her
       husband because he is so much older
   (3) that she cannot go back in time and
       change the course of her life
   (4) that she must leave her husband and
       start a new life
   (5) that she can never bear children

3. What do Dorothea's questions in lines 23–25, "Was it her fault that she had believed in him—had believed in his worthiness?—And what, exactly, was he?" reveal about her marriage?

   (1) Dorothea's husband had lied about his education.
   (2) Dorothea has misjudged her husband and is now unsure of his true character.
   (3) Dorothea blames herself for her unhappy marriage.
   (4) Dorothea's wedding ring is worth far more than she had thought.
   (5) Dorothea pities her husband because he is ill.

4. With which choice would Dorothea probably agree?

   (1) Marriage ensures a blissful love life.
   (2) Married people should never admit to themselves that they are unhappy.
   (3) Marital problems are easy to solve when you are just beginning marriage.
   (4) It is not important to find worth in the person to whom you are married.
   (5) It is possible for married people to grow apart until they are almost strangers.

5. Earlier in the novel, Dorothea decides to marry a well-educated man against her family's wishes because she hopes to learn from him.

   Based on this information and the excerpt, what has happened between Dorothea and her husband?

   (1) Her family was wrong about the marriage.
   (2) She has learned a great deal from her husband.
   (3) She has learned more than her husband.
   (4) Her husband has turned out to be a disappointment.
   (5) She has more lessons to learn from him.

Questions 6–11 are based on the following passage.

WHAT DECISION DOES HAL HAVE TO MAKE?

As though understanding his thoughts, Hal Winters spoke up. "Well, has it been worthwhile? What about it, eh? What about marriage and all that?" he asked and then

5 laughed. Hal tried to keep on laughing but he too was in an earnest mood. He began to talk earnestly. "Has a fellow got to do it?" he asked. "Has he got to be harnessed up and driven through like a horse?"

10 Hal didn't wait for an answer but sprang to his feet and began to walk back and forth between the corn shocks. He was getting more and more excited. Bending down suddenly he picked up an ear of the yellow

15 corn and threw it at the fence. "I've got Nell Gunther in trouble," he said. "I'm telling you, but keep your mouth shut."

Ray Pearson arose and stood staring. He was almost a foot shorter than Hal, and

20 when the younger man came and put his two hands on the older man's shoulders they made a picture. There they stood in the big empty field with the quiet corn shocks standing in rows behind them and the red

25 and yellow hills in the distance, and from being just two indifferent workmen they had become all alive to each other. Hal sensed it and because that was his way he laughed. "Well, old daddy," he said awkwardly,

30 "come on, advise me. I've got Nell in trouble. Perhaps you've been in the same fix yourself. I know what everyone would say is the right thing to do, but what would you say? Shall I marry and settle down? Shall I

35 put myself into the harness to be worn out like an old horse? You know me, Ray. There can't anyone break me but I can break myself. Shall I do it or shall I tell Nell to go to the devil? Come on, you tell me.

40 Whatever you say, Ray, I'll do."

—Excerpted from *Winesburg, Ohio*
by Sherwood Anderson

6. What is the setting of the passage?

    (1) a stable
    (2) a cornfield
    (3) a factory
    (4) a stockyard
    (5) a racetrack

7. What current social problem is discussed in the passage?

    (1) teenage marriages
    (2) single-parent families
    (3) unwanted pregnancies
    (4) troubled marriages
    (5) child support

8. What is Hal describing in lines 34–36 when he says, "Shall I put myself into the harness to be worn out like an old horse"?

    (1) horse breeding
    (2) retirement
    (3) farmwork
    (4) marriage
    (5) jockeys

9. What other choice could the way the narrator's use of language to describe Hal and Ray standing together (lines 18–27) best be compared to?

    (1) a poem
    (2) a movie
    (3) a sculpture
    (4) a play
    (5) a painting

10. Why does Hal seek Ray's advice?

    (1) Ray is Hal's father.
    (2) Ray has the same problem.
    (3) Hal respects Ray's opinion.
    (4) Ray evaluates situations impersonally.
    (5) Hal has no other friends.

11. Near the end of the story, Hal decides to marry Nell Gunther without waiting to hear Ray's opinion.

    Based on this information and the excerpt, what can you infer helped Hal make his decision?

    (1) his parents' marriage
    (2) Ray's good example
    (3) fear of Nell's anger
    (4) societal pressure
    (5) legal consequences

Questions 12–17 are based on the following passage.

WHAT KIND OF PLACE IS SLEEPY HOLLOW?

The immediate cause, however, of the prevalence of supernatural stories in these parts, was doubtless owing to the vicinity of Sleepy Hollow. There was a contagion in the
5 very air that blew from that haunted region; it breathed forth an atmosphere of dreams and fancies infecting all the land. Several of the Sleepy Hollow people were present at Van Tassel's, and, as usual, were doling out
10 their wild and wonderful legends. Many dismal tales were told about funeral trains, and mourning cries and wailings heard and seen about the great tree where the unfortunate Major André was taken, and
15 which stood in the neighborhood. Some mention was made also of the woman in white, that haunted the dark glen at Raven Rock, and was often heard to shriek on winter nights before a storm, having
20 perished there in the snow. The chief part of the stories, however, turned upon the favorite spectre of Sleepy Hollow, the headless horseman, who had been heard several times of late, patrolling the country,
25 and who, it was said, tethered the horse nightly among the graves in the churchyard.

—Excerpted from "The Legend of Sleepy Hollow"
by Washington Irving

12. What is the narrator's purpose in the introductory sentence of this passage?

(1) to explain a process
(2) to contrast different settings
(3) to state a cause-and-effect relationship
(4) to classify types of stories
(5) to compare fiction with nonfiction

13. How could the atmosphere of Sleepy Hollow best be described?

(1) wild and wonderful
(2) dreamlike and fanciful
(3) mournful and dismal
(4) infected and contagious
(5) unfortunate and horror-stricken

14. What can you conclude about the residents of Sleepy Hollow?

They are
(1) terrified
(2) uneducated
(3) hysterical
(4) diseased
(5) superstitious

15. What was the favorite story recounted at Van Tassel's?

The story about
(1) the woman in white
(2) the funeral trains
(3) the headless horseman
(4) the haunted rock
(5) Major André

16. What kind of TV program do you think the residents of Sleepy Hollow would have found most interesting?

(1) a soap opera
(2) a science fiction show
(3) a documentary
(4) a music video
(5) a game show

17. Major John André was a British spy who was hanged by American forces during the American Revolution.

What does this information provide to the story?

(1) It adds to the historical atmosphere.
(2) It makes the story realistic.
(3) It supports the supernatural mood.
(4) It helps to characterize the residents.
(5) It attempts to name the headless horseman.

Questions 18–22 are based on the following passage.

WHY IS ASKENOV FALSELY ACCUSED OF A CRIME?

An official and two soldiers got out of the carriage. The official went up to Askenov and asked him who he was and where he was from. Askenov told him what he wanted
5 to know and asked if he would like to join him for tea. But the official continued to question him: "Where did you sleep last night? Were you alone or with a merchant? Did you see the merchant in the morning?
10 Why did you leave the inn so early?" Askenov wondered why he was being asked these things. He told him all that had occurred, then added, "But why are you questioning me like this? I'm not some kind
15 of thief or bandit. I am traveling on my own business, and there's nothing for you to question me about."

Then the official called a soldier and said: "I am the district police officer, and I
20 am asking you these questions because the merchant you stayed with last night has been found with his throat cut. Show me your things. Search him."

They went into the cabin, took out his
25 suitcase and bag, untied them and began to search. Suddenly, the officer pulled out a knife from the bag and shouted:

"Whose knife is this?"

Askenov looked. He saw that they had
30 found a knife covered with blood in his bag, and he was frightened.

"And why is there blood on the knife?"

Askenov wanted to answer, but he could not speak.

35 "I ... I don't know ... I ... knife ... I, not mine ... "

Then the officer said: "In the morning they found a merchant with his throat cut. There is no one besides you who could have
40 done it. The cabin was locked from the inside. You have in your bag a knife covered with blood, and, in fact, guilt is written all over your face. Now tell us, how did you kill

him and how much money did you steal?"

45 Askenov swore that he did not do it, that he had not seen the merchant since they had drunk tea together, that the only money he had was his own eight thousand rubles, that the knife was not his.

—Excerpted from "God Sees the Truth, but Waits"
by Leo Tolstoy

18. What was the most incriminating evidence against Askenov?

  (1) Guilt was written all over his face.
  (2) Askenov drank tea with the merchant.
  (3) The cabin was locked from the inside.
  (4) A blood-covered knife was found in his bag.
  (5) He had eight thousand rubles.

19. Which statement best summarizes the action occurring in this scene?

  (1) A suspect is questioned about a murder.
  (2) A criminal refuses to cooperate with police.
  (3) Two soldiers assist a district police officer.
  (4) A police officer forces a suspect to plead guilty.
  (5) A merchant is brutally murdered and robbed.

20. What is the author's purpose in writing the dialogue, "I ... I don't know ... I ... knife ... I, not mine ..." (lines 35–36) in this way?

To show that
  (1) Askenov suffers from a chronic stuttering problem
  (2) Askenov is lying to the police officer
  (3) Askenov's nervousness is affecting his speech
  (4) Askenov has a limited vocabulary
  (5) Askenov is a poor conversationalist

21. To whose behavior could the police officer in this scene best be compared?

  (1) a defense attorney
  (2) a jury member
  (3) a judge
  (4) a prosecuting attorney
  (5) an eyewitness

22. Earlier in the story Askenov's wife dreams that her husband, a young, fair, curly-headed man, will return home again as an old man with grey hair.

Based on this information and the excerpt, what can you infer will happen to Askenov after this scene?

He will
(1) return to his home
(2) go to prison
(3) take a long journey
(4) prove his innocence
(5) find the guilty person

Answers are on pages 104–105.

The excerpts on pages 42–46 are from works written between 1920 and 1960.

Questions 1–6 are based on the following passage.

WHAT DOES LAURIE'S MOTHER OBSERVE ABOUT HER SON?

The day my son Laurie started kindergarten he renounced corduroy overalls with bibs and began wearing blue jeans with a belt; I watched him go off the first morning
5 with the older girl next door, seeing clearly that an era of my life was ended, my sweet-voiced nursery-school tot replaced by a long-trousered, swaggering character who forgot to stop at the corner and wave good-
10 bye to me. He came home the same way, the front door slamming open, his cap on the floor, and the voice suddenly become raucous shouting, "Isn't anybody here?"

At lunch he spoke insolently to his
15 father, spilled his baby sister's milk, and remarked that his teacher said we were not to take the name of the Lord in vain.

"How was school today?" I asked, elaborately casual.

20 "All right," he said.

"Did you learn anything?" his father asked.

Laurie regarded his father coldly. "I didn't learn nothing," he said.

25 "Anything," I said. "Didn't learn anything."

"The teacher spanked a boy, though," Laurie said, addressing his bread and butter. "For being fresh," he added, with his mouth
30 full.

"What did he do?" I asked. "Who was it?"

Laurie thought. "It was Charles," he said. "He was fresh. The teacher spanked him and made him stand in a corner. He was
35 awfully fresh."

"What did he do?" I asked again, but Laurie slid off his chair, took a cookie, and left, while his father was still saying, "See here, young man."

—Excerpted from "Charles" by Shirley Jackson

1. How is the information in the introductory paragraph structured?

    (1) to classify styles of little boys' clothing
    (2) to compare and contrast changes in Laurie's behavior
    (3) to explain why mothers are overprotective of their sons
    (4) to analyze the effects of nursery school on children
    (5) to record the stages of early childhood development

2. What is the main topic of conversation between Laurie and his parents?

    (1) his day in school
    (2) his classmate's behavior
    (3) his teacher's strictness
    (4) his incorrect grammar
    (5) his fresh manners

3. Which of the following words does *not* accurately describe Laurie's behavior in this passage?

    (1) independent
    (2) rebellious
    (3) inattentive
    (4) sweet
    (5) rude

4. What is Laurie doing while his father is saying, "See here, young man" (lines 38–39)?

    (1) slamming the door
    (2) leaving the room
    (3) spilling his sister's milk
    (4) staring at his snack
    (5) throwing down his cap

5. Which of the following people would be most qualified to analyze the personality of a five-year-old?

    (1) a mother
    (2) a father
    (3) a kindergarten teacher
    (4) a child psychologist
    (5) a school principal

6. A reviewer stated that the author of this passage created stories in which every human being has a devil and an angel inside. Often in daily life, others fail to see the evil personality.

    Based on this review and Laurie's words and actions, what can you infer about Laurie when asked by his father who Charles is?

    (1) He is trying to protect Charles.
    (2) He is the student the teacher punished.
    (3) He really doesn't know who Charles is.
    (4) He is just avoiding a talk with his father.
    (5) He invented the situation in the classroom.

Questions 7–12 are based on the following passage.

WHAT ARE THE CHARACTER'S CAREER PLANS?

I was sitting in church one day and a Brother Nachin asked me how I was doing work-wise.

I looked up at Brother Nachin, who
5 because he was nearly six feet tall, was a giant among Puerto Ricans. He carried himself like an athlete—gently but with authority. Although he was thirty-four, he moved like a twenty-year-old. What was
10 striking about him were his red hair and green eyes. When he spoke there was hardly a trace of a Puerto Rican accent. He had been born in the States like me.

"I'm still working at the same old job." I
15 frowned.

"Good money?" he smiled.

"Good money? I don't ever expect to get rich there."

"Listen, would you like to work in a
20 bakery?"

"I don't know how to bake," I smiled.

"You don't have to. There's other work there. Porter, packer, and you can work yourself up. If you'd like, I'll take you to the
25 union."

Uhm, I thought. But I said, "I'm willing. How about next week? I'd have to give notice at my two jobs."

"Next week." He smiled.

30 "Next week."

—Excerpted from *Savior, Savior, Hold My Hand*
by Piri Thomas

7. What attitude toward Brother Nachin does the author reveal through descriptive language?

  (1) fear
  (2) gentleness
  (3) admiration
  (4) holiness
  (5) jealousy

8. Where does the conversation between Brother Nachin and the narrator take place?

  (1) in a bakery
  (2) in an employment agency
  (3) in a packing plant
  (4) in a labor union
  (5) in a church

9. Why does the author use the word *giant* (line 6)?

To emphasize Brother Nachin's
  (1) authority
  (2) height
  (3) athletic skill
  (4) fame
  (5) striking appearance

10. How does the narrator feel about his current job?

  (1) unhappy
  (2) fearful
  (3) successful
  (4) challenged
  (5) unknowledgeable

11. Which of the following statements best expresses the main idea of the passage?

  (1) Brother Nachin is actively involved in labor union activities.
  (2) Brother Nachin is a leader in the Puerto Rican community.
  (3) Brother Nachin wants to help the narrator get a job in a bakery.
  (4) The narrator doesn't expect to get rich from his job.
  (5) Both Brother Nachin and the narrator were born in America.

12. The author's works deal with the discrimination that immigrants and minorities experience in both the workplace and society.

Based on this information and the passage, where do you think the narrator expects to find some hope?

  (1) his current jobs
  (2) his family
  (3) the government
  (4) the labor union
  (5) the Puerto Rican community

Questions 13–19 are based on the following passage.

WHAT DO YOU LEARN ABOUT GEORGE?

George Stoyonovich was a neighborhood boy who had quit high school on an impulse when he was sixteen, run out of patience, and though he was ashamed
5　everytime he went looking for a job, when people asked him if he had finished and he had to say no, he never went back to school. This summer was a hard time for jobs and he had none. Having so much time on his
10　hands, George thought of going to summer school, but the kids in his classes would be too young. He also considered registering in a night high school, only he didn't like the idea of the teachers always telling him what
15　to do. He felt that they had not respected him. The result was he stayed off the streets and in his room most of the day. He was close to twenty and had needs with the neighborhood girls, but no money to spend,
20　and he couldn't get more than an occasional few cents because his father was poor, and his sister Sophie, who resembled George, a tall bony girl of twenty-three, earned very little and what she had she kept for herself.
25　Their mother was dead, and Sophie had to take care of the house.

Very early in the morning George's father got up to go to work in a fish market. Sophie left about eight for her long ride in
30　the subway to a cafeteria in the Bronx. George had his coffee by himself, then hung around in the house. When the house, a five-room railroad flat above a butcher store, got on his nerves he cleaned it up—mopped the
35　floors with a wet mop and put things away. But most of the time he sat in his room.

—Excerpted from "A Summer's Reading"
by Bernard Malamud

13. Why didn't George enroll in summer school?

  (1)　He was busy looking for a summer job.
  (2)　He thought that the teachers were disrespectful.
  (3)　The other students would be too young.
  (4)　He didn't like taking orders.
  (5)　He was upset about being a dropout.

14. What is the main purpose of the passage?

  (1)　to compare George with his sister
  (2)　to establish the story's setting
  (3)　to summarize George's family conflicts
  (4)　to discuss the problems of unemployment
  (5)　to summarize George's background

15. Why does George want to earn money?

  (1)　to date the neighborhood girls
  (2)　to pay for his night school tuition
  (3)　to rent his own apartment
  (4)　to supplement his sister's income
  (5)　to hire a private tutor

16. What does George usually do during the daytime?

  (1)　He roams the streets.
  (2)　He stays in his room.
  (3)　He plans his return to school.
  (4)　He looks for a job.
  (5)　He works as a janitor.

17. What would a career counselor most likely say to George?

  (1)　"Apply for unemployment compensation."
  (2)　"Start your own business."
  (3)　"Improve your interviewing skills."
  (4)　"Consult a lawyer about job discrimination."
  (5)　"Get a high school diploma."

18. What does the writing style used in the passage most closely resemble?

  (1)　a newspaper editorial
  (2)　a job application letter
  (3)　an employee's evaluation
  (4)　a biography
  (5)　a high school textbook

19. George later tells a lie to a man, falsely claiming to have read 100 books. The man tells the neighbors who praise George for trying to improve himself.

Based on this information and the passage, what can you infer was important to George?

(1) hard work
(2) self worth
(3) education
(4) family
(5) friendship

Answers are on pages 105–106.

The excerpts on pages 46–51 are from works written after 1960.

Questions 1–5 are based on the following passage.

WHY IS A POLICEMAN TRAILING TWO MEN?

Leon shook me. "He's behind us—the cop's following us!" I looked back and saw the red light on top of the car whirling around, and I could make out the dark
5 image of a man, but where the face should have been there were only the silvery lenses of the dark glasses he wore.

"Stop, Leon! He wants us to stop!"

Leon pulled over and stopped on the
10 narrow gravel shoulder.

"What in the hell does he want?" Leon's hands were shaking.

Suddenly the cop was standing beside the truck, gesturing for Leon to roll down
15 the window. He pushed his head inside, grinding the gum in his mouth; the smell of Doublemint was all around us.

"Get out. Both of you."

I stood beside Leon in the dry weeds
20 and tall yellow grass that broke through the asphalt and rattled in the wind. The cop studied Leon's driver's license. I avoided his face—I knew that I couldn't look at his eyes, so I stared at his black half-Wellingtons, with
25 the black uniform cuffs pulled over them;

but my eyes kept moving, upward past the black gun belt. My legs were quivering and I tried to keep my eyes away from his. But it was like the time when I was very little and
30 my parents warned me not to look into the masked dancers' eyes because they would grab me, and my eyes would not stop.

"What's your name?" His voice was high-pitched and it distracted me from the
35 meaning of the words.

I remember Leon said, "He doesn't understand English so good," and finally I said that I was Antonio Sousea, while my eyes strained to look beyond the silver
40 frosted glasses that he wore; but only my distorted face and squinting eyes reflected back.

And then the cop stared at us for a while, silent; finally he laughed and chewed
45 his gum some more slowly. "Where were you going?"

"To Grants." Leon spoke English very clearly. "Can we go now?"

Leon was twisting the key chain around
50 his fingers, and I felt the sun everywhere. Heat swelled up from the asphalt and when cars went by, hot air and motor smell rushed past us.

"I don't like smart guys, Indians ... ."

—Excerpted from *Tony's Story* by Leslie Marmon Silko

1. From whose point of view is the story told?

   (1) Leon's
   (2) the cop's
   (3) Antonio's
   (4) the author's
   (5) two Indians'

2. What are the "half-Wellingtons" (line 24)?

   (1) handcuffs
   (2) boots
   (3) trousers
   (4) dark glasses
   (5) guns

3. What social problem is addressed?

   (1) literacy
   (2) racial prejudice
   (3) police brutality
   (4) drunken driving
   (5) illegal aliens

4. How do Leon and Antonio react to the police officer?

   (1) warmly
   (2) confidently
   (3) impolitely
   (4) nervously
   (5) dishonestly

5. Why does the narrator find the officer's speech distracting?

   (1) The officer chomped on chewing gum.
   (2) The officer's voice was high-pitched.
   (3) The officer spoke in English.
   (4) The officer's sunglasses had mirrored lenses.
   (5) The officer laughed while he spoke.

Questions 6–10 are based on the following passage.

HOW DOES AURORA REACT TO HER DAUGHTER'S PREGNANCY?

"Just pregnant!" Aurora cried, confusion turning suddenly to rage. "You ... negligent." But words failed her, and to Emma's intense annoyance she began to
5 smite her forehead with the back of her hand. Aurora had been raised in an era of amateur theatricals and was not without her stock of tragic gestures. She continued to smite her forehead vigorously, as she always
10 did when she was very upset, wincing each time at the pain it gave her hand.

"Stop that," Emma cried, standing up. "Stop smiting your goddamn forehead, Momma! You know I hate that!"

15 "And I hate you," Aurora cried, abandoning all reason. "You're not a thoughtful daughter! You never have been a thoughtful daughter! You never will be a thoughtful daughter!"

"What did I do?" Emma yelled,
20 beginning to cry. "Why can't I be pregnant? I'm married."

Aurora struggled to her feet and faced her daughter, meaning to show her such scorn as she had never seen before. "You
25 may call this marriage but I don't," she yelled. "I call it squalor!"

"We can't help it!" Emma said. "It's all we can afford."

Aurora's lip began to tremble. Scorn got
30 lost—everything was lost. "Emma, it's not the point ... you shouldn't have ... it's not the point at all," she said, suddenly on the verge of tears.

"What's the point then?" Emma said.
35 "Just tell me. I don't know."

"Mee!" Aurora cried, with the last of her fury. "Don't you see? My life is not settled. Me!"

Emma winced, as she always did when
40 her mother cried "Mee!" at the world. The sound was as primitive as a blow. But as her mother's chin began to shake and pure fury began its mutation into pure tearfulness, she understood a little and put out her arm.

45 "Who will I ever ... get now?" Aurora cried. "What man would want a grandmother? If you could ... have waited ... then I might have ... got somebody."

—Excerpted from *Terms of Endearment*
by Larry McMurtry

6. What happens when Aurora gets upset?

   (1) She curses her daughter.
   (2) She becomes speechless.
   (3) She acts confused.
   (4) She hits her forehead.
   (5) She cries uncontrollably.

7. What is the main reason for Aurora's anger about Emma's pregnancy?

   (1) Emma's husband can't afford to support a child.
   (2) Men will find Aurora undesirable because she's a grandmother.
   (3) Emma didn't ask her mother's permission to get pregnant.
   (4) Emma and her husband will be negligent parents.
   (5) Emma is not settled enough to become a mother.

8. At the end of the passage, how does Emma feel about her mother's outburst?

   (1) guilty
   (2) scornful
   (3) sympathetic
   (4) annoyed
   (5) apologetic

9. Why is the dialogue in the passage effective?

   Because it
   (1) presents the conflict from Emma's point of view
   (2) reveals how unwanted pregnancies cause marital problems
   (3) shows Emma's lack of consideration for her mother
   (4) realistically dramatizes the argument between Aurora and Emma
   (5) imitates how most mothers speak to their daughters

10. What could Aurora's role in this scene best be compared to?

    An actress's performance in
    (1) a horror movie
    (2) a soap opera
    (3) a TV talk show
    (4) an adventure series
    (5) a situation comedy

Go to **www.GEDReading.com** for additional practice and instruction!

Questions 11–16 are based on the following passage.

WHAT DOES SQUEAKY, THE NARRATOR, SAY ABOUT CYNTHIA?

Now some people like to act like things come easy to them, won't let on that they practice. Not me. I'll high-prance down 34th Street like a rodeo pony to keep my knees
5 strong even if it does get my mother uptight so that she walks ahead like she's not with me, don't know me, is all by herself on a shopping trip, and I am somebody else's crazy child. Now, you take Cynthia Proctor for instance.
10 She's just the opposite. If there's a test tomorrow, she'll say something like, "Oh, I guess I'll play handball this afternoon and watch television tonight," just to let you know she ain't thinking about the test. Or like last
15 week when she won the spelling bee for the millionth time, "A good thing you got 'receive,' Squeaky, cause I would have got it wrong. I completely forgot about the spelling bee." And she'll clutch the lace on her blouse
20 like it was a narrow escape. Oh, brother. But of course when I pass her house on my early morning trots around the block, she is practicing the scales on the piano over and over and over and over. Then in music class
25 she always lets herself get bumped around so she falls accidentally on purpose onto the piano stool and is so surprised to find herself sitting there that she decides just for fun to try out the ole keys. And what do you know—
30 Chopin's waltzes just spring out of her fingertips and she's the most surprised thing in the world. A regular prodigy. I could kill people like that. I stay up all night studying the words for the spelling bee. And you can
35 see me any time of the day practicing running.

—Excerpted from "Raymond's Run" by Toni Cade Bambara

11. Which word would Squeaky probably use to describe Cynthia?

(1) hypocritical
(2) modest
(3) lazy
(4) honest
(5) shy

12. What major point does Squeaky express in this passage?

(1) Most people easily admit their shortcomings.
(2) Some people pretend that they make their accomplishments effortlessly.
(3) People born with artistic talents are lucky.
(4) Some people constantly complain about their inadequacies.
(5) Gifted people are conceited and brag about their accomplishments.

13. Why are the details in the passage arranged the way they are?

(1) to classify types of students
(2) to analyze the causes of competition
(3) to compare and contrast two characters
(4) to analyze the effects of hard work
(5) to explain the process of learning

14. What does Squeaky mean when she says that she prances down the street "like a rodeo pony" (line 4)?

(1) Her legs are as muscular as a horse's.
(2) She parades down the street to show off her legs.
(3) She raises her knees as she walks.
(4) She wears flashy clothes to attract attention.
(5) She rehearses her role in the cattle roundup.

15. What can you conclude that Squeaky would like to be?

(1) a pianist
(2) a comedian
(3) an actress
(4) an A student
(5) a track star

16. What is the tone of the passage?

(1) humorous
(2) serious
(3) bitter
(4) sympathetic
(5) indirect

Questions 17–21 are based on the following passage.

WHAT HAPPENS DURING
A GAME OF CATCH?

   I had decided to become a professional
baseball player. I had bought a Louisville
Slugger, a ball, and a first baseman's mitt. I
asked my father to play catch with me one
5 Sunday afternoon, but he refused. My
mother must have overheard this
conversation, because she called him to her
room, where they quarrelled. In a little while,
he came out to the garden and asked me to
10 throw the ball to him. What happened then
was ridiculous and ugly. I threw the ball
clumsily once or twice and missed the
catches he threw to me. Then I turned my
head to see something—a boat on the river.
15 He threw the ball, and it got me in the nape
of the neck and stretched me out
unconscious in my grandfather's ruined
garden. When I came to, my nose was
bleeding and my mouth was full of blood.
20 I felt that I was being drowned. My father
was standing over me. "Don't tell your
mother about this," he said. When I sat up
and he saw that I was all right, he went
down through the garden toward the barn
25 and the river.

—Excerpted from "The National Pastime"
by John Cheever

17. Where are the father and the son playing
catch?

   (1) by a riverbank
   (2) in a barn
   (3) in an empty lot
   (4) in a park
   (5) in a garden

18. How does the son look when he plays
catch?

   (1) professional
   (2) ridiculous
   (3) ugly
   (4) clumsy
   (5) fair

19. Why is the sentence "I felt that I was being
drowned" (line 20) effective?

   (1) It emphasizes the boy's physical
       sensation of bleeding.
   (2) It suggests the boy's fear of swimming
       underwater.
   (3) It implies that the mother emotionally
       suffocates her son.
   (4) It shows that the father's power is
       overwhelming.
   (5) It depicts the boy's nightmare while he
       was unconscious.

20. What is the most significant event described
in the passage?

   (1) The son bought new baseball
       equipment.
   (2) The mother overheard her son's
       conversation.
   (3) The mother and father quarreled with
       each other.
   (4) The son was hit in the neck with a
       baseball.
   (5) The father went for a long walk.

21. Why does the father say to his son, "Don't
tell your mother about this" (lines 21–22)?

   (1) His wife disapproves of playing baseball.
   (2) He thinks his wife will become angry
       again.
   (3) He likes to share secrets with his son.
   (4) His wife faints at the sight of blood.
   (5) He's certain that his wife will punish
       their son.

Answers are on pages 106–107.

Chapter 3

Poetry

GED Language Arts, Reading pages 217–247
Complete GED pages 615–636

Questions 1–6 are based on the following poem.

WHAT DOES AN AIRPLANE PASSENGER THINK ABOUT?

Poem

Seven thousand feet over
The American Midwest
In the black and droning night
Sitting awake and alone
5 I worry the stewardess.
Would you like some coffee, sir?
How about a magazine?
No thanks. I smile and refuse.
My father died today. I
10 Fifteen hundred miles away
Left at once for home, having
received the news from my mother
In tears on the telephone.
He never rode on a plane.

              —Ted Berrigan

1. What emotional effect is conveyed through the poem's language?

(1) sadness
(2) anger
(3) boredom
(4) insensitivity
(5) tension

2. What can you conclude that the speaker in the poem is going to attend?

(1) a news conference
(2) a family reunion
(3) a funeral
(4) a business meeting
(5) a Mother's Day party

3. Why does the stewardess seem worried?

(1) The droning airplane engine signals engine problems.
(2) Evening flights make her feel uneasy.
(3) She senses that the speaker is upset.
(4) She wonders if the pilot can stay awake.
(5) She is inexperienced in handling passengers.

4. What is the main purpose of the poem?

(1) to reveal the mother's overemotional personality
(2) to depict the speaker's homesickness and loneliness
(3) to explain why the speaker's father never rode in a plane
(4) to describe the sky from an airline passenger's viewpoint
(5) to express the speaker's reaction to his father's death

5. Who is speaking in lines 6 and 7?

(1) another passenger
(2) the stewardess
(3) the poet
(4) the speaker's mother
(5) the pilot

6. A reviewer remarked that one of this poet's talents was his ability to present a speaker whom the reader would find likeable and funny.

Based on this information and the poem, what makes the speaker likeable?

His realization that
(1) he didn't want coffee
(2) his father had never flown
(3) he worried the stewardess
(4) he had been away from home
(5) he didn't like airplanes

Questions 7–11 are based on the following poem.

WHAT DOES THE POET REMEMBER ABOUT ABRAHAM LINCOLN?

P. S. 42

I learned in grammar school
that Lincoln walked many miles for a book
which he read lying on his stomach
before a bubbling-kettle fireplace
5 That's how I wanted to read a book!
So as soon as the class was over
I hurried a mile from my neighborhood
    library
    to another library
10 Of course they wouldn't issue me a card
"Use the library in your own
    neighborhood"
So I stole my book
and late that night
15 under my blanket with a little flashlight
I read
And I do not exaggerate when I say
I fully felt the joy that was Lincoln's
                                    —Gregory Corso

7. What is the purpose of the poem?

(1) to highlight biographical details from Lincoln's life
(2) to justify stealing books from the public library
(3) to show the value of an elementary school education
(4) to explain how Lincoln inspired the poet's love of reading
(5) to criticize librarians' treatment of school-aged children

8. How are the details in the poem arranged?

(1) to trace the process of checking out a library book
(2) to analyze the effects of self-education
(3) to classify types of studying methods
(4) to explain why children enjoy reading
(5) to compare and contrast two ways of reading a book

9. Why didn't the poet select a book from his neighborhood library?

(1) Another library had a more interesting collection of books.
(2) He wanted to imitate Lincoln by walking a long distance for a book.
(3) His neighborhood library closed when his class was over.
(4) Like Lincoln, he wanted to explore places away from home.
(5) He wanted to apply for a card at another library.

10. Why does the poet include the image "a little flashlight" (line 15)?

(1) to mirror the image of Lincoln's reading by the light of a fireplace
(2) to suggest that the poet is trying to conserve electricity
(3) to show that light is a poetic symbol for awareness and discovery
(4) to create a vivid image of something secret and forbidden
(5) to imply that reading with a flashlight causes eye strain

11. What information about Lincoln's life would the poet probably not study in grammar school?

(1) Lincoln was assassinated at Ford's Theater.
(2) Lincoln worked as a rail-splitter.
(3) Lincoln experienced bouts of emotional depression.
(4) Lincoln abolished the institution of slavery.
(5) Lincoln practiced law in Springfield, Illinois.

Questions 12–16 are based on the following poem.

WHAT DOES A BOY DISCOVER ABOUT HIS FATHER'S JOB?

The Miracle Factory

Papa's got a job in a miracle-factory
downtown someplace, one of those streets
west of the avenue, in an old
5 building taller than God. There's a marble lobby, two
elevators behind brass gates, a newsstand,
and a draft whenever anyone pushes through
10   the glass revolving doors. Upstairs
after the corridor, damp, windy cold
RING BELL COME IN the loft
looks at an airshaft. Soot settles softly, like
15   snow.
I went there once with Papa. Standing soldierly
put out my hand to the boss, said, How d'you do.
20 I didn't like it much. The boss said, Boy,
when you grow up I want you to remember
making miracles is just like any other line, profit and loss,
25 also supply and demand. You got to sell
the product, make them believe
in it! He shook my hand.
Papa said later, He's the boss, without
the boss, no factory. Remember that.
—Constance Urdang

12. From whose point of view is the poem told?

(1) the father's
(2) the boss's
(3) the poet's
(4) the elevator operator's
(5) the boy's

13. What is unique about the factory?

(1) It has a marble lobby.
(2) It is located in a skyscraper.
(3) It manufactures miracles.
(4) Its employees are overjoyed.
(5) It always makes huge profits.

14. What is the best explanation for the meaning of "Soot settles softly, like/snow" (lines 14–15)?

(1) The factory is located in a cold climate.
(2) The windows were open during a blizzard.
(3) The factory is covered with powdery dust.
(4) The soot in the factory is white and flaky.
(5) The factory resembles a ski resort.

15. In which of the following would you most likely find the situation in the poem?

(1) a horror movie
(2) a science fiction story
(3) a preacher's sermon
(4) a labor union meeting
(5) a TV comedy

16. What does the boss's dialogue (lines 20–27) reveal about him?

(1) his extraordinary advertising campaign
(2) his approach to operating a business
(3) his respect for his customers
(4) his impressive sales record
(5) his concern for his employees

Questions 17–21 are based on the following poem.

WHAT DOES THE SPEAKER UNDERSTAND ABOUT HIMSELF?

Alone

From childhood's hour I have not been
As others were—I have not seen
As others saw—I could not bring
My passions from a common spring—
5 From the same source I have not taken
My sorrow—I could not awaken
My heart to joy at the same tone—
And all I lov'd—I lov'd alone—
Then—in my childhood—in the dawn
10 Of a most stormy life—was drawn
From ev'ry depth of good and ill
The mystery which binds me still—
From the torrent, or the fountain—
From the red cliff of the mountain—
15 From the sun that 'round me roll'd
In its autumn tint of gold—
From the lightning in the sky
As it pass'd me flying by—
From the thunder, and the storm—
20 And the cloud that took the form
(When the rest of heaven was blue)
Of a demon in my view.

—Edgar Allen Poe

17. Which choice best describes the speaker's overall tone in the poem?

(1) acceptance
(2) anger
(3) denial
(4) joy
(5) bitterness

18. Which of these situations is most like the speaker's?

(1) a soldier going into battle
(2) an office worker attending a meeting
(3) an athlete playing with his or her team
(4) a soloist performing with an orchestra
(5) a weather forcaster making a prediction

19. What is the speaker's purpose in the poem?

To emphasize his
(1) life of luxury
(2) conformity
(3) lack of feeling
(4) intelligence
(5) peculiarity

20. Which choice best explains what the poet refers to in, "The mystery which binds me still—(line 12)"?

He felt that
(1) he had experienced many personal griefs
(2) he was the only person who understood his feelings
(3) he could not understand why he was talented
(4) he could not explain the purpose of life
(5) he had learned from his childhood how to be happy

21. When he was very young, the speaker of the poem lost his beloved mother and father and the woman who adopted him and showed him love. He struggled with his adopted father for most of his life.

Based on this information and the poem, how do you think the speaker felt after the loss of his loved ones?

(1) angry
(2) solitary
(3) confused
(4) inspired
(5) comforted

Questions 22–26 are based on the following poem.

WHAT HAPPENED ON
WILSON RIVER ROAD?

Traveling Through the Dark

Traveling through the dark I found a deer
dead on the edge of Wilson River road.
It is usually best to roll them into the
canyon:
5 that road is narrow; to swerve might make
more dead.

By glow of the tail-light I stumbled back of
the car
and stood by the heap, a doe, a recent
10 killing;
she had stiffened already, almost cold.
I dragged her off; she was large in the
belly.

My fingers touching her side brought me
15 the reason—
her side was warm; her fawn lay there
waiting,
alive, still, never to be born.
Beside that mountain road I hesitated.

20 The car aimed ahead its lowered parking
lights;
under the hood purred the steady engine.
I stood in the glare of the warm exhaust
turning red;
25 around our group I could hear the
wilderness listen.

I thought hard for us all—my only
swerving,
then pushed her over the edge into the
30 river.
—William Stafford

22. When does the event described in the poem occur?

(1) in the early morning
(2) in the late morning
(3) in the early afternoon
(4) in the late afternoon
(5) in the evening

23. What kind of language is used in the poem?

(1) figurative
(2) sarcastic
(3) formal
(4) descriptive
(5) analytical

24. What does the phrase "she was large in the belly" (lines 12–13) reveal about the deer?

She was
(1) overfed
(2) old
(3) pregnant
(4) dead
(5) cold

25. Which word best describes the speaker's attitude toward animals?

(1) respectful
(2) cautious
(3) annoyed
(4) brutal
(5) religious

26. Who would most likely identify with the sentiment expressed in the poem?

(1) hunters
(2) wildlife preservationists
(3) truck drivers
(4) farmers
(5) animal trainers

Questions 27–30 are based on the following passage.

WHAT EVENT OCCURRED IN A MOTHER'S HOUSE?

The Toy Bone

Looking through boxes
in the attic at my mother's house in
    Hamden,
I find a model airplane, snapshots
5 of a dog wearing baby clothes,
a catcher's mitt—the oiled
pocket eaten
by mice—and I discover
the toy bone, the familiar smell of it.

10 I sat alone each day
after school, in the living room
of my parents' house in Hamden, ten
years old, eating
slices of plain white bread.
15 I listened to the record, Connie
Boswell singing
again and again, her voice
turning like a heel, "The Kerry Dancers,"
and I knew she was crippled, and sang
20 from a wheelchair. I played
with Tommy, my red-and-white
Shetland collie, throwing
    his toy bone
into the air and catching it, or letting it
25   fall,
while he watched me
with intent, curious eyes.
I was happy
in the room with shades drawn.

—Donald Hall

27. What is the setting of the first stanza (lines 1–9)?

(1) the baby's room
(2) the backyard
(3) the baseball field
(4) the attic
(5) the living room

28. How did the speaker feel about playing with his dog?

(1) intent
(2) curious
(3) happy
(4) alone
(5) bored

29. On what relationship does the poem focus?

The one between
(1) a fan and a singer
(2) a mother and a child
(3) a husband and a wife
(4) a father and a son
(5) a boy and a pet

30. Why is the description of Connie's "voice/turning like a heel" (lines 17 and 18) effective?

(1) The speaker liked to tap his feet to the rhythm of the song.
(2) The image of her lively voice sharply contrasts with the description of her handicap.
(3) She was singing the background music for a dance performance.
(4) The image of her moving feet implies that she wasn't seriously crippled.
(5) Her singing dramatically changes the atmosphere of the setting.

Questions 31–36 are based on the following poem.

HOW DOES THE SPEAKER FEEL ABOUT HER FATHER?

Without Title
—*for my Father who lived without ceremony*

It's hard you know without the buffalo,
the shaman*, the arrow
but my father went out each day to hunt
as though he had them.
5 He worked in the stockyards.
All his life he brought us meat.
No one marked his first kill,
no one sang his buffalo song.
Without a vision he had migrated to the
10 city
and went to work in the packing house.
When he brought home his horns and
  hides
my mother said
15 get rid of them.
I remember the animal tracks of his car
out the drive in snow and mud,
the aerial on his old car waving
like a bow string.
20 I remember the silence of his lost power,
the red buffalo painted on his chest.
Oh, I couldn't see it
but it was there, and in the night heard
his buffalo grunts like a snore.

—Diane Glancy

*shaman: a tribal medicine man or priest

31. What is the speaker referring to with the words *to hunt* (line 3)?

Her father's
(1) search for his ancestors
(2) love for his wife and child
(3) pursuit of financial goals
(4) work to earn his wages
(5) attempts to gain his daughter's love

32. What word best describes the tone of the poem?

(1) sorrowful
(2) respectful
(3) humorous
(4) angry
(5) unfeeling

33. What is the speaker referring to in lines 7 and 8?

(1) a trial
(2) a journey
(3) a business
(4) an animal
(5) an initiation

34. What choice is the best explanation of the father's occupation?

(1) butcher
(2) game hunter
(3) taxidermist
(4) truck driver
(5) nature guide

35. How is the poem organized?

(1) examples of the father's love for his family
(2) comparison of the father's dreams to real life
(3) causes of the father's unhappiness in his job
(4) list of the daily routine of the speaker's father
(5) justification of the importance of hard work

36. The poet's own father had been forced by his wife to give up the ceremonial traditions of his Cherokee tribe when he moved to the city.

Based on this information and the poem, what does the speaker realize about herself?

She is
(1) more realistic than her father
(2) more suited to the life in the city
(3) in agreement with her mother
(4) like her father in love of tradition
(5) unable to understand her father's past

Questions 37–41 are based on the following poem.

HOW DID LORD RANDAL'S SWEETHEART BETRAY HIM?

Lord Randal

"O where have you been, Lord Randal, my
    son?
O where have you been, my handsome
    young man?"—
5 "I have been to the wild wood; mother make
    my bed soon,
For I'm weary with hunting, and fain would
    lie down."

"Who gave you your dinner, Lord Randal, my
10   son?
Who gave you your dinner, my handsome
    young man?"—
"I dined with my sweetheart; mother, make
    my bed soon,
15 For I'm weary with hunting, and fain would
    lie down."

"What had you for dinner, Lord Randal, my
    son?
What had you for dinner, my handsome young
20   man?"—
"I had eels in broth; mother, make my bed
    soon,
For I'm weary with hunting and fain would
    lie down."

25 "And where are your bloodhounds, Lord
    Randal, my son?
And where are your bloodhounds, my
    handsome young man?"—
"O they swelled and they died; mother, make
30   my bed soon,
For I'm weary with hunting, and fain would
    lie down."

"O I fear you are poisoned, Lord Randal, my
    son!
35 O I fear you are poisoned, my handsome
    young man!"—
"O yes! I am poisoned; mother, make my bed
    soon,
For I'm sick at the heart, and fain would lie
40   down."

—Author unknown

37. Which of the following statements best summarizes the major event described in the poem?

  (1) A hunter's bloodhounds mysteriously die.
  (2) A young man wants his mother to make his bed.
  (3) A young man eats dinner with his sweetheart.
  (4) A young man is poisoned by his girlfriend.
  (5) A mother asks her son about his activities.

38. What does "sick at the heart" (line 39) refer to?

Lord Randal's
  (1) fear that his mother will die
  (2) passion for his sweetheart
  (3) depression at being betrayed
  (4) sickly nature since birth
  (5) fatigue from hunting all day

39. Which of the following modern formats would be most effective in using the situation portrayed in this poem?

  (1) a TV crime show
  (2) a science fiction story
  (3) a family movie
  (4) an adventure film
  (5) a romantic comedy

40. What is the overall structure of the first four stanzas of the poem?

  (1) analyses of cause-and-effect relationships
  (2) dialogue consisting of questions and answers
  (3) comparisons of two characters' viewpoints
  (4) explanations of a hunter's weariness
  (5) descriptions of a mother-and-son relationship

41. In popular tradition, this song is about a young nobleman who died between the years 1200 and 1300.

Based on this information and the events in the poem, what is the most likely explanation why the person who murdered Lord Randal would go unpunished?

(1) Nobility could not be punished for crimes.
(2) Lord Randal deserved his punishment.
(3) The means of his death could not be proved.
(4) The criminal could easily hide from the law.
(5) A lover was assumed to be innocent.

Questions 42–46 are based on the following poem.

WHAT PROBLEM PLAGUES THE TOWNSPEOPLE?

Hamelin Town's in Brunswick
  By famous Hanover city;
    The river Weser, deep and wide,
    Washes its wall on the souther side;
5   A pleasanter spot you never spied:
  But, when begins my ditty,
    Almost five hundred years ago,
    To see the townsfolk suffer so
  From vermin was a pity.

10 Rats!
  They fought the dogs, and kill'd the cats,
    And bit the babies in the cradles,
  And ate the cheeses out of the vats,
    And lick'd the soup from the cook's own
15   ladles,
  Split open the kegs of salted sprats,
  Made nests inside men's Sunday hats,
  And even spoil'd the women's chats,
    By drowning their speaking
20 With shrieking and squeaking
  In fifty different sharps and flats.

—Excerpted from "The Pied Piper of Hamelin"
by Robert Browning

42. Where does the poem take place?

(1) Brunswick
(2) Hamelin Town
(3) Southern Side
(4) Weser
(5) Hanover

43. What is the main idea of the second stanza (lines 10–21)?

(1) Rats fight and kill cats.
(2) Rats are a menace to babies.
(3) Rats like to eat cheese.
(4) Rats are a destructive nuisance.
(5) Rats make high pitched sounds.

44. Why does the poet use rhyme throughout the excerpt?

(1) to create a lively, musical effect
(2) to poke fun at children's nursery rhymes
(3) to establish a serious tone
(4) to emphasize the figurative language
(5) to imply that poetry is superior to prose

45. To which of the following insects could the portrayal of rats in the poem best be compared?

(1) moths
(2) spiders
(3) cockroaches
(4) bees
(5) butterflies

46. Later in the poem, the town's council hires a piper who rids the town of all its rats; however, the last line of the poem reads as follows: "If we've promised them [those who rid the town of rats] ought, let us keep our promises."

Based on this line, what can you infer most likely happened between the piper and the town council?

(1) The council failed to pay.
(2) The rats returned to town.
(3) The town suffered from another pest.
(4) The piper failed to do his job.
(5) The council honored its contract.

Questions 47–51 are based on the following poem.

WHAT DO MARY AND WARREN DISCUSS ABOUT SILAS?

Mary sat musing on the lamp-flame at the
    table,
Waiting for Warren. When she heard his
    step,
5 She ran on tip-toe down the darkened
    passage
To meet him in the doorway with the news
And put him on his guard. "Silas is back."
She pushed him outward with her through
10   the door
And shut it after her. "Be kind," she said.
She took the market things from Warren's
    arms
And set them on the porch, then drew him
15   down
To sit beside her on the wooden steps.
"When was I ever anything but kind to
    him?
But I'll not have the fellow back," he said.
20 "I told him so last haying, didn't I?
'If he left then,' I said, 'that ended it.'
What good is he? Who else will harbor
    him
At his age for the little he can do?
25 What help he is there's no depending on.
Off he always goes when I need him the
    most ..."
—Excerpted from "The Death of the Hired Man"
by Robert Frost

47. Why does Mary meet her husband Warren in the doorway?

(1) to greet him affectionately
(2) to guard against dangerous intruders
(3) to help him with the groceries
(4) to persuade him to sit on the steps
(5) to caution him about Silas's return

48. Which word would Warren probably use to describe Silas?

(1) senile
(2) kind
(3) unreliable
(4) good
(5) dependable

49. What can you conclude is the setting of the poem?

(1) a market
(2) a barn
(3) a nursing home
(4) a pasture
(5) a farmhouse

50. What do the techniques that the poet uses to develop the poem most closely resemble?

(1) a script
(2) a song
(3) a ghost story
(4) a short story
(5) an editorial

51. Later in the poem, Mary says to Warren, "Home is the place where, when you have to go there, They have to take you in."

Based on this line how do you think Warren will deal with Silas?

(1) He will continue to be angry.
(2) He will ignore Mary's pleas.
(3) He will tell Silas to leave.
(4) He will find work on another farm.
(5) He will soften his resentment.

Questions 52–56 are based on the following poem.

WHAT HAPPENS WHEN THE SOLDIER DIES?

Death of the Soldier

Life contracts and death is expected,
As in a season of autumn.
The soldier falls.

He does not become a three-days'
5   personage,
Imposing his separation,
Calling for pomp.

Death is absolute and without memorial,
As in a season of autumn,
10 When the wind stops.

When the wind stops and, over the
   heavens,
The clouds go, nevertheless,
In their direction.

             —Wallace Stevens

52. Which choice is the best explanation for the word "falls" in line 3?

(1) stumbles
(2) dies
(3) retreats
(4) strikes
(5) fails

53. Which word best describes the tone of the poem?

(1) violent
(2) angry
(3) sentimental
(4) somber
(5) pompous

54. To which of the following does the poet compare death?

(1) war
(2) clouds
(3) heaven
(4) wind
(5) autumn

55. Which statement best expresses one other central message of the poem?

(1) Memorial ceremonies honoring dead soldiers are meaningless.
(2) Most soldiers in active combat expect to die heroically.
(3) History proves that war is brutal and senseless.
(4) Death is part of a natural cycle and an expected condition of war.
(5) Whenever a soldier dies, the wind stops blowing.

56. The poet wrote this poem after his mother's death; however, he was writing about a new kind of death being experienced on the battlefields of World War I in 1915.

Based on this information and the poem, what can you infer was the poet's attitude about the soldier's death?

It was
(1) completely justified in war time
(2) worthy of a nation's sorrow
(3) natural that he died for his country
(4) acceptable in modern society
(5) unnatural in cutting a life short

Answers are on pages 107–110.

Questions 1–4 are based on the following passage.

HOW DOES CAPTAIN DAVENPORT INVESTIGATE THE MURDER OF SERGEANT WATERS?

ELLIS: *(loud)* Private Wilkie!

WILKIE: *(offstage)* Yes, sir! *(Almost immediately, WILKIE appears in the doorway. He is dressed in a proper*
5 *uniform of fatigues, boots, and cap.)*

ELLIS: Cap'n wants to see you!

WILKIE: Yes indeedy! *(moves quickly to the table, where he comes to attention and salutes)* Private James Wilkie
10 reporting as ordered, sir.

DAVENPORT: At ease, Private. Have a seat. *(To ELLIS as WILKIE sits)* That will be all, Corporal.

ELLIS: Yes, sir.

15 ELLIS salutes and exits. DAVENPORT waits until he leaves before speaking.

DAVENPORT: Private Wilkie, I am Captain Davenport—

WILKIE: *(interjecting)* Everybody knows
20 that, sir. You all we got down here. *(smiles broadly)* I was on that first detail got your quarters togetha', sir.

(DAVENPORT nods.)

DAVENPORT: *(coldly)* I'm conducting an
25 investigation into the events surrounding Sergeant Waters' death. Everything you say to me will go into my report, but that report is confidential.

WILKIE: I understand, sir.

30 DAVENPORT *removes pad and pencil from briefcase.*

DAVENPORT: How long did you know Sergeant Waters?

WILKIE: 'Bout a year, sir. I met him last
35 March—March 5th—I remember the date, I had been staff sergeant exactly two years the day after he was assigned. This company was basically a baseball team then, sir. See, most of the boys had played
40 for the Negro League, so naturally the army put us all together. *(chuckles at the memory)* We'd be assigned to different companies—Motor Pool—Dump Truck— all week long—made us do the dirty work
45 on the post—garbage, clean-up—but on Saturdays we were whippin' the hell out of 'em on the baseball diamond! I was hittin' .352 myself! And we had a boy, C. J. Memphis? He coulda' hit a ball from Fort
50 Neal to Berlin, Germany—or Tokyo—if he was battin' right-handed. *(pauses, catches DAVENPORT'S impatience)* Well, the army sent Waters to manage the team. He had been in Field's Artillery—Gunnery
55 Sergeant. Had a Croix de Guerre from the First War, too.

DAVENPORT: What kind of man was he?

WILKIE: All spit and polish, sir.

—From *A Soldier's Play* by Charles Fuller

1. If Captain Davenport were a civilian, which of the following jobs would he most likely hold?

   (1) teacher
   (2) psychologist
   (3) baseball manager
   (4) warden
   (5) lawyer

2. Which word best describes the captain's conduct during the interview?

   (1) businesslike
   (2) disrespectful
   (3) high-pressured
   (4) unprofessional
   (5) disorganized

3. Why are the stage directions *pauses, catches DAVENPORT'S impatience* (lines 51–52) effective?

   Because they suggest that
   (1) Captain Davenport has a short attention span
   (2) Private Wilkie knows he is discussing details unrelated to the murder
   (3) Captain Davenport disapproves of army baseball teams
   (4) army captains are intolerant of privates
   (5) Private Wilkie's tone of voice is irritating

4. According to Private Wilkie, how can Captain Davenport's presence at the army base best be characterized?

   (1) confidential
   (2) unnoticed
   (3) well-known
   (4) dangerous
   (5) unexpected

Questions 5–9 are based on the following passage.

WHY IS LENNY UPSET WITH HER SISTER MEG?

BABE: Lenny, what's wrong? What's the matter?

LENNY: It's Meg! I could just wring her neck! I could just wring it!

5 BABE: Why? Wha'd she do?

LENNY: She lied! She sat in that hospital room and shamelessly lied to Old Granddaddy. She went on telling such untrue stories and lies.

10 BABE: Well, what? What did she say?

LENNY: Well, for one thing she said she was gonna have a RCA record coming out with her picture on the cover, eating pineapples under a palm tree.

15 BABE: Well, gosh Lenny, maybe she is! Don't you think she really is?

LENNY: Babe, she sat here this very afternoon and told me how all that she's done this whole year is work as a clerk for a dog
20 food company.

BABE: Oh, shoot. I'm disappointed.

LENNY: And then she goes on to say that she'll be appearing on the "Johnny Carson Show" in two weeks' time. Two weeks'
25 time! Why, Old Granddaddy's got a TV set right in his room. Imagine what a letdown it's gonna be.

BABE: Why, mercy me.

LENNY: *(slamming the coffeepot on)* Oh,
30 and she told him the reason she didn't use the money he sent her to come home Christmas was that she was right in the middle of making a huge multi-million motion picture and was just under too
35 much pressure.

BABE: My word!

LENNY: The movie's coming out this spring. It's called "Singing in a Shoe Factory." But she only has a small leading
40 role—not a large leading role.

BABE: (laughing) For heaven's sake—

LENNY: I'm sizzling. Oh, I just can't help it! I'm sizzling!

BABE: Sometimes Meg does such strange
45 things.

LENNY: (slowly, as she picks up the opened box of birthday candy) Who ate this candy?

BABE: (hesitantly) Meg.

50 LENNY: My one birthday present, and look what she does! Why, she's taken one little bite out of each piece and then just put it back in! Ooh! That's just like her! That is just like her!

55 BABE: Lenny, please—

LENNY: I can't help it! It gets me mad! It gets me upset! Why, Meg's always run wild—she started smoking and drinking when she was fourteen years old, she
60 never made good grades—never made her own bed! But somehow she always seemed to get what she wanted.

—Excerpted from *Crimes of the Heart*
by Beth Henley

5. What has Meg been doing during the past year?

She has been
(1) a guest on the "Johnny Carson Show"
(2) an actress in a major motion picture
(3) a clerk in a dog food company
(4) an executive with RCA
(5) a supervisor in a shoe factory

6. Why does the playwright include the stage direction *slamming the coffeepot on* (line 29)?

To show Lenny's
(1) hospitality
(2) clumsiness
(3) thirst
(4) anger
(5) strength

7. Why is Lenny's concluding dialogue (lines 56–62) effective?

(1) It explains the reasons behind Lenny's attitude toward Meg.
(2) It proves that wild teenagers grow up to be maladjusted adults.
(3) It illustrates why poor students have behavior problems.
(4) It emphasizes Lenny's disapproval of smoking and drinking.
(5) It suggests that most sisters develop unhappy relationships.

8. What can you infer from the scene?

(1) Babe resents Lenny's criticism of Meg.
(2) Babe is dissatisfied with her life.
(3) Babe finds Meg's fantasies believable.
(4) Babe encourages Lenny's criticism of Meg.
(5) Babe wishes Meg were famous.

9. In the play, the playwright reveals that Babe's character is a person who craves candy and sweets.

What might this information suggest about the stage directions for Babe in line 49, *hesitantly*?

Babe is
(1) angry that Lenny didn't share her candy
(2) guilty because she really took the bites of candy
(3) sad that Lenny dislikes their sister Meg
(4) unsure who is responsible for eating the candy
(5) amused that only bites were eaten from the candy

Questions 10–14 are based on the following passage.

HOW DOES JOE FEEL ABOUT HIS CAREER?

JOE: Doris, I was a big operator at one time.

WIFE: That was fifteen years ago, Joe.

5　JOE: All right, the bottom fell out of the real-estate market. I went broke. All right. I still got it up here … *(indicates his head)* I can't think in terms of thirty-six hundred dollars a year. I'm not a candy-store owner, keeping an eye on the kids so they
10　won't steal the pennies off the newsstand. I'm a business man …

WIFE: Joe, how many businesses have you tried? You tried the trucking business. You tried the…

15　JOE: I was out of my element. I'm a builder. This is my racket.

WIFE: I won't let you take any more money off that girl.

JOE: What do you want me to do?
20　You want me to take this job as a lousy building inspector?

WIFE: Joe, don't talk so loud.

JOE: You want me to walk around with my hand out, waiting for a five-dollar pay-
25　off? I won't do it. Some of the biggest men in the business are my friends.

WIFE: All right, Joe, sit down. Don't be so excited. *(Joe, who has risen from his bed, now sinks back, his breath coming heavily.)*

30　JOE: *(looking down at his knees)* Don't worry so about me, Doris. We're not going to take another penny off that girl. If you don't think it sticks me in my heart to ask her for ten dollars here, fifteen dollars
35　there, so I can play a little pinochle. Don't you think I have a little contempt for myself? I don't have to be reminded. I love that girl. What have I ever given her?

—Excerpted from *The Big Deal* by Paddy Chayefsky

10. If Joe were reading the job listings in a newspaper, what type of job would he most likely apply for?

　(1) a building custodian
　(2) an architect
　(3) a construction worker
　(4) a building contractor
　(5) a real estate agent

11. Where does this scene takes place?

　(1) in a living room
　(2) in a home office
　(3) in a bedroom
　(4) in a newsstand
　(5) in a candy store

12. Which word best represents Joe's feelings about asking his daughter for money?

　(1) pride
　(2) self-contempt
　(3) indifference
　(4) anger
　(5) gratitude

13. Which phrase best accounts for Joe's dissatisfaction with his current job situation?

　It stems from his
　(1) preoccupation with the past
　(2) wife's interference
　(3) friends' discouragement
　(4) lack of experience
　(5) lazy attitude

14. Why does the playwright include stage directions in this scene?

　To explain
　(1) the characters' backgrounds
　(2) Doris's movements
　(3) the stage setting
　(4) Joe's tone of voice
　(5) Joe's gestures

Questions 15–20 are based on the following passage.

HOW IS WILLIE'S CAMPAIGN FOR GOVERNOR PROGRESSING?

SADIE: You know, suppose they told him. He might go on making speeches. Even if he found out he was a sucker.

JACK: Maybe.

5 SADIE: God, aren't they awful?

(STARK, in shirtsleeves, enters, and hesitates in embarrassment.)

JACK: Hey, look. It's Willie. Come on in, Willie. Give Willie a drink.

10 SADIE: He don't take it.

JACK: Oh, yeah. Have a seat, Willie.

STARK: No, thanks, Jack. No, thanks.

JACK: What's on your mind?

STARK: *(standing aimlessly)* Nothing.
15 Nothing special.

JACK: Come on, spill it.

STARK: It's just—it's just I wondered.

JACK: Wondered what?

STARK: How do you think it's going?

20 JACK: What's going?

STARK: My campaign.

JACK: I think it's going fine, Willie.

STARK: They didn't seem to be listening so good yesterday.

25 JACK: You tell 'em too much. It breaks down their brain cells.

STARK: Looks like they'd want to hear about my road program. And my tax program.

JACK: Just say you're going to soak the
30 rich.

STARK: What this state needs is a balanced tax program. Now, the ratio between income and—

JACK: We heard the speech.

35 SADIE: *(speaking to him over her shoulder as she refills her glass)* Hell, make 'em laugh. Make 'em cry. Stir 'em up. They aren't alive, most of them, and haven't been in twenty years. *(moving toward*
40 *him, warming to the topic)* Hell, their wives have lost their shape, likker won't set on their stomach, and they've lost their religion, so it's up to you to stir 'em up. Make 'em feel alive again. For half an hour.
45 They'll love you for it. Hell, heat 'em up.

STARK: I've heard that kind of talk.

SADIE: It's no secret. It gets around.

STARK: Maybe I can't talk that way.

JACK: That's the only way you'll ever be
50 Governor.

—Excerpted from *All the King's Men*
by Robert Penn Warren

15. What does Jack mean by, "It breaks down their brain cells" (lines 25–26)?

(1) Concentration causes physical changes in the brain.
(2) Most of the voters in the state are mentally slow.
(3) Listening to Willie's speeches causes brain disorders.
(4) Willie breaks down his speeches into several topics.
(5) Willie overloads his audience with information.

16. Which word best describes the language of Sadie's dialogue?

(1) formal
(2) delicate
(3) indirect
(4) informal
(5) sympathetic

17. What kind of political candidate is Willie?

(1) ruthless
(2) experienced
(3) shrewd
(4) naive
(5) dynamic

18. Which of the following would Sadie probably recommend as a model for Willie's speeches?

(1) a newscaster's commentary
(2) a revivalist preacher's sermon
(3) a U.S. president's inaugural address
(4) a stand-up comedian's monologue
(5) a tax lawyer's lecture

19. What role does Jack play in the scene?

(1) Sadie's boyfriend
(2) Willie's advisor
(3) Sadie's business partner
(4) a detached observer
(5) Willie's political opponent

20. Willie Stark loses this campaign, but later in the play he runs again for governor and wins.

What can you infer that Willie learned about political campaigning?

(1) Voters will always elect the most popular candidate.
(2) Political candidates must tell the truth.
(3) Candidates need to understand their opponents.
(4) Candidates have to make informational speeches.
(5) Voters want to be inspired rather than receive a lot of information.

Questions 21–26 are based on the following passage.

WHAT DO TWO SISTERS DISCUSS WITH EACH OTHER?

LOTTIE: Oh. Well, don't be gone long. We've got to get started back soon.

CORA: Oh, please don't talk about going.

LOTTIE: My God, Cora, we can't stay here
5 all night. *(She peers out the window now, wondering about Morris.)* Morris is funny, Cora. Sometimes he just gets up like that and walks away. I never know why. Sometimes he's gone for hours at a time.
10 He says the walk helps his digestion, but I think it's because he just wants to get away from me at times. Did you ever notice how he is with people? Like tonight. He sat there when all the young people were here,
15 and he didn't say hardly a word. His mind was a thousand miles away. Like he was thinking about something. He seems to be always thinking about something.

CORA: Morris is nice to you. You've got
20 no right to complain.

LOTTIE: He's nice to me … in some ways.

CORA: Good heavens, Lottie! He gave you those red patent-leather slippers, and that fox neckpiece … you should be grateful.

25 LOTTIE: I know, but … there's some things he hasn't given me.

CORA: Lottie! That's not his fault. You've got no right to hold that against him!

LOTTIE: Oh, it's just fine for you to talk.
30 You've got two nice kids to keep you company. What have I got but a house full of cats?

CORA: Lottie, you always claimed you never wanted children.

35 LOTTIE: Well … what else can I say to people?

CORA: *(This is something of a revelation to her.)* I just never knew.

—Excerpted from *The Dark at the Top of the Stairs* by William Inge

21. What upsets Lottie most about her marriage to Morris?

    (1) He hasn't made her pregnant.
    (2) He bribes her with gifts.
    (3) He acts unsociably.
    (4) He always seems distracted.
    (5) He avoids her company.

22. What is Cora's role throughout most of the scene?

    (1) to support Lottie
    (2) to withhold her opinion
    (3) to defend Morris
    (4) to cause an argument
    (5) to criticize Morris

23. What is Morris's excuse for walking?

    (1) his need for privacy
    (2) his digestion
    (3) his discomfort with Lottie
    (4) his shopping trips
    (5) his desire to think

24. What character trait does Lottie reveal in this scene?

    (1) calmness
    (2) secretiveness
    (3) loyalty
    (4) generosity
    (5) gratefulness

25. With whom should Lottie and Morris probably discuss their problems?

    (1) a divorce lawyer
    (2) a pediatrician
    (3) Cora's husband
    (4) an advice columnist
    (5) a marriage counselor

26. Why are the stage directions in lines 37–38, *This is something of a revelation to her,* effective?

Because they
    (1) suggest that Cora is simpleminded
    (2) imply that understanding is a religious experience
    (3) show that Cora has misjudged Lottie's feelings
    (4) explain Cora's stage movements and facial expressions
    (5) create tension in the dramatic action

Questions 27–31 are based on the following passage.

WHAT IS EMILY'S MOTHER THINKING ABOUT?

(The lights are brought up on the living room of the Crews' home. Elizabeth Crews is there, crying. Emily comes in.)

EMILY: Mother, what is it? Has something
5 happened to Daddy?

ELIZABETH: No. He's in bed asleep.

EMILY: Then what is it?

ELIZABETH: Inez blessed me out and stopped speaking to me over last night.
10 She says we've ruined the boy's whole vacation. You've broken his heart, given him all kinds of complexes and he's going home tomorrow …

EMILY: But I saw him at the drugstore
15 tonight and I had a long talk with him and he said he understood …

ELIZABETH: But Inez doesn't understand. She says she'll never forgive either of us again. *(She starts to cry.)*

20 EMILY: Oh, Mother. I'm sorry …

ELIZABETH: Emily, if you'll do me one favor … I promise you I'll never ask another thing of you again as long as I live. And I will never nag you about going
25 out with Leo again as long as I live …

EMILY: What is the favor, Mother?

ELIZABETH: Let that boy take you to the dance day after tomorrow …

EMILY: Now, Mother …

30 ELIZABETH: Emily. I get down on my knees to you. Do me this one favor … *(a pause)* Emily … Emily … *(She is crying again.)*

EMILY: Now, Mother, please. Don't cry. I'll
35 think about it. I'll call Leo and see what he says. But please don't cry like this … Mother … Mother … *(She is trying to console her as the lights fade.)*

—Excerpted from *The Dancers* by Horton Foote

27. Which choice best describes Emily's mother?

She is
(1) angry
(2) ashamed
(3) teasing
(4) funny
(5) unconcerned

28. Who can you infer Leo is?

Emily's
(1) father
(2) brother
(3) boyfriend
(4) cousin
(5) uncle

29. What action will Emily take based on the dialogue?

(1) go to the dance
(2) hide in her room
(3) ask her father's advice
(4) ignore her mother
(5) leave with friends

30. Who could best identify with Emily's problem?

(1) a mother with daughters
(2) a favorite grandmother
(3) an adolescent male
(4) a school counselor
(5) an eighteen-year-old female

31. Earlier in the play, Elizabeth tells Inez's brother that Emily was ill; however, Emily didn't want to go to the dance with him.

Based on this information and the excerpt, what choice best describes Emily's actions?

(1) thoughtful
(2) inconsiderate
(3) mature
(4) vengeful
(5) sincere

Questions 32–37 are based on the following passage.

WHAT DO YOU NOTICE ABOUT THE RELATIONSHIP BETWEEN BLANCHE AND HER SISTER STELLA?

STELLA: You never did give me a chance to say much, Blanche. So I just got in the habit of being quiet around you.

BLANCHE: *(vaguely)* A good habit to get
5 into … *(then abruptly)* You haven't asked me how I happened to get away from the school before the spring term ended.

STELLA: Well, I thought you'd volunteer that information—if you wanted to tell me.

10 BLANCHE: You thought I'd been fired?

STELLA: No, I—thought you might have resigned …

BLANCHE: I was so exhausted by all I'd been through my—nerves broke.
15 *(nervously tamping cigarette)* I was on the verge of lunacy, almost! So Mr. Graves—Mr. Graves is the high school superintendent— he suggested I take a leave of absence. I couldn't put all of those details into the
20 wire … *(She drinks quickly.)* Oh, this buzzes right through me and feels so good!

STELLA: Won't you have another?

BLANCHE: No, one's my limit.

STELLA: Sure?

25 BLANCHE: You haven't said a word about my appearance.

STELLA: You look just fine.

BLANCHE: God love you for a liar! Daylight never exposed so total a ruin. But
30 you—you've put on some weight, you're just as plump as a little partridge! And it's so becoming to you!

STELLA: Now, Blanche—

BLANCHE: Yes, it is or I wouldn't say it!
35 You just have to watch around the hips a little. Stand up.

STELLA: Not now.

BLANCHE: You hear me? I said stand up. *(Stella complies reluctantly.)*

—Excerpted from *A Streetcar Named Desire*
by Tennessee Williams

32. Why has Blanche left her high school teaching assignment?

    (1) She resigned.
    (2) She was fired.
    (3) She is on vacation.
    (4) She took a leave of absence.
    (5) She found another job.

33. For what purpose does the playwright use stage directions in lines 15 and 20?

    To describe Blanche's
    (1) tone of voice
    (2) gestures
    (3) physical appearance
    (4) private thoughts
    (5) position on the stage

34. Whose advice should Blanche probably seek?

    The advice of
    (1) a high school superintendent
    (2) a beautician
    (3) a psychiatrist
    (4) a nurse
    (5) a job counselor

35. Why does Blanche compare Stella to a partridge?

    (1) because Stella is nervous as a bird
    (2) because Stella has a feathery hairstyle
    (3) because Stella's appetite is as small as a bird's
    (4) because Stella has gained some weight
    (5) because Stella is much smaller than Blanche

36. Which word best describes Blanche's behavior as revealed in her concluding line of dialogue (line 38)?

(1) childish
(2) bossy
(3) vicious
(4) helpful
(5) reluctant

37. Later the playwright reveals that Blanche was dismissed from her teaching job for inappropriate behavior.

Based on this information and Stella's dialogue in lines 11–12, "No, I—thought you might have—resigned . . . ," what can you infer are Stella's thoughts about Blanche?

She thinks that
(1) Blanche works too hard
(2) she and Blanche are alike
(3) Blanche needs another job
(4) her sister needs counseling
(5) the superintendent is unfair

Questions 38–42 are based on the following passage.

HOW DO TWO MEN VIEW ROMANCE AND LOVE?

ALGERNON: My dear fellow, the way you flirt with Gwendolyn is perfectly disgraceful. It is almost as bad as the way Gwendolyn flirts with you.

5 JACK: I am in love with Gwendolyn. I have come up to town expressly to propose to her.

ALGERNON: I thought you had come up for pleasure? … I call that business.

10 JACK: How utterly unromantic you are!

ALGERNON: I really don't see anything romantic in proposing. It is very romantic to be in love. But there is nothing romantic about a definite proposal. Why, one may
15 be accepted. One usually is, I believe. Then the excitement is all over. The very essence of romance is uncertainty. If I ever get married, I'll certainly try to forget the fact.

JACK: I have no doubt about that, dear
20 Algy. The Divorce Court was specially invented for people whose memories are so curiously constituted.

ALGERNON: Oh! There is no use speculating on that subject. Divorces are
25 made in Heaven—*(JACK puts out his hand to take a sandwich. ALGERNON at once interferes.)* Please don't touch the cucumber sandwiches. They are ordered specially for Aunt Augusta. *(takes one and eats it)*

30 JACK: Well, you have been eating them all the time.

ALGERNON: That is quite a different matter. She is my aunt. *(takes plate from below)* Have some bread and butter. The
35 bread and butter is for Gwendolyn. Gwendolyn is devoted to bread and butter.

JACK: *(advancing to table and helping himself)* And very good bread and butter
40 it is too.

ALGERNON: Well, my dear fellow, you need not eat as if you were going to eat it all. You behave as if you were married to her already. You are not married to her
45 already, and I don't think you will ever be.

JACK: Why on earth do you say that?

ALGERNON: Well, in the first place, girls never marry the men they flirt with. Girls don't think it right.

50 JACK: Oh, that is nonsense!

ALGERNON: It isn't. It is a great truth. It accounts for the extraordinary number of bachelors that one sees all over the place. In the second place, I don't give my
55 consent.

JACK: Your consent!

ALGERNON: My dear fellow, Gwendolyn is my first cousin.

—Excerpted from *The Importance of Being Earnest* by Oscar Wilde

38. Why does Jack say to Algernon, "How utterly unromantic you are" (line 10)?

Because Algernon
(1) thinks that flirting is disgraceful
(2) views love as a foolish emotion
(3) is a confirmed bachelor who refuses to marry
(4) is bitter because of the high divorce rates
(5) believes that proposing marriage is business, not pleasure

39. Which of the following words accurately describes Algernon?

(1) affectionate
(2) loyal
(3) unbiased
(4) opinionated
(5) sympathetic

40. What do the stage directions referring to Jack describe?

(1) his lovesickness
(2) his movements toward food
(3) his resentful attitude
(4) his hospitality
(5) his awkwardness

41. Given Algernon's style of conversation, at what type of occasion would his presence probably be appreciated most?

(1) at a dinner with a group of conservative widows
(2) at a picnic with his teenage nieces and their mothers
(3) at a wedding reception
(4) at a club for sophisticated young men
(5) at a fundraising party for a Christian charity

42. Later in the play, Algernon falls in love with Jack's ward, Cecily, and his actions are the opposite of his words in this passage. He goes to great lengths to get her to accept his proposal of marriage.

Based on this information and Algernon's dialogue in this passage, what change has taken place regarding Algernon's views on marriage?

(1) He still finds marriage as a boring and imperfect union.
(2) He now believes that people must marry within their own class.
(3) He continues to disapprove of romance in a marriage.
(4) He comes to accept that love continues and grows after marriage.
(5) He begins to see marriage as a means of improving social status.

Questions 43–48 are based on the following passage.

WHOM IS LOPAKHIN EXPECTING?

(A room that is still called the nursery. One of the doors leads into ANYA's room. Dawn; the sun will soon rise. It is May, the cherry trees are in bloom, but it is cold in the
5 *orchard; there is a morning frost. The windows in the room are closed. Enter DUNYASHA with a candle, and LOPAKHIN with a book in his hand.)*

LOPAKHIN: The train is in, thank God.
10 What time is it?

DUNYASHA: Nearly two. *(blows out the candle)* It's already light.

LOPAKHIN: How late is the train, anyway? A couple of hours at least. *(yawns and*
15 *stretches)* I'm a fine one! What a fool I've made of myself! Came here on purpose to meet them at the station, and then overslept … Fell asleep in the chair. It's annoying … You might have waked me.

20 DUNYASHA: I thought you had gone. *(listens)* They're coming now, I think!

LOPAKHIN: *(listens)* No … they've got to get the luggage now … She's a fine person. Sweet-tempered, simple. I remember when I
25 was a boy of fifteen, my late father—he had a shop in the village then—gave me a punch in the face and made my nose bleed … We had come into the yard here for some reason or other, and he'd had a drop too much.
30 Lyubov Andreyevna—I remember as if it were yesterday—still young, and so slender, led me to the washstand in this very room, the nursery. "Don't cry, little peasant," she said, "it will heal in time for your wedding."
35 *(pause)* Little peasant … my father was a peasant, it's true, and here I am in a white waistcoat and tan shoes. Like a pig in a pastry shop … I may be rich, I've made a lot of money, but if you think about it, analyze it,
40 I'm a peasant through and through. *(turning pages of the book)* Here I've been reading this book, and I didn't understand a thing. Fell asleep over it.

—Excerpted from *The Cherry Orchard*
by Anton Chekhov

43. Approximately when does this scene take place?

    (1) sunrise
    (2) late morning
    (3) 2:00 A.M.
    (4) 2:00 P.M.
    (5) midnight

44. Why is Lopakhin annoyed that he overslept?

    (1) He was in the middle of reading a book.
    (2) He was supposed to meet visitors at the train station.
    (3) Dunyasha forgot to wake him up.
    (4) He was planning a trip abroad and missed the train.
    (5) He was supposed to cook breakfast.

45. What is the main topic of Lopakhin's concluding dialogue (lines 22–43)?

    (1) his fight with his drunken father
    (2) his love of literature
    (3) his anxiety about his wedding
    (4) his fond memories of Lyubov Andreyevna
    (5) his successful business career

46. Why does Lopakhin compare himself to "a pig in a pastry shop" (lines 37–38)?

    (1) Despite his wealth, he still feels like a peasant.
    (2) When he goes to the bakery, he buys too many sweet desserts.
    (3) His white waistcoat accentuates his weight problems.
    (4) He is self-conscious about his sloppy appearance and bad manners.
    (5) He is greedy for money and hoards his expensive possessions.

47. What element of fiction does the playwright show in the paragraph in parentheses preceding the dialogue (lines 1–8)?

    (1) characterization
    (2) theme
    (3) point of view
    (4) conflict in plot
    (5) setting

48. In the third act Lopakhin buys the estate with the cherry orchard after its aristocratic owner, Lyubnov Andreyevna, loses her fortune. She and her upper class friends react resentfully to Lopakhin's purchase of the estate.

Based on the passage, what can you infer is the basis of this resentment?

(1) Lopahkin has always been disliked by the owner.
(2) Lopahkin was previously poor while Andreyevna was rich.
(3) Lopahkin used money gained illegally to buy the estate.
(4) Lopahkin bought the estate to marry the owner's daughter.
(5) Lopahkin planned to evict the owner and her friends.

Go to **www.GEDReading.com** for additional practice and instruction!

Questions 49–54 are based on the following passage about trials that occurred in Salem, Massachusetts in the 1600s in which people were accused of being witches.

WHY WON'T JOHN PROCTOR SURRENDER HIS SIGNED CONFESSION?

DANFORTH: *(considers; then with dissatisfaction)* Come, then, sign your testimony. *(to Cheever)* Give it to him. *(Cheever goes to Proctor, the confession*
5 *and pen in hand. Proctor does not look at it.)* Come, man, sign it.

PROCTOR: *(after glancing at the confession)* You have all witnessed it— it is enough.

10 DANFORTH: You will not sign it?

PROCTOR: You have all witnessed it; what more is needed?

DANFORTH: Do you sport with me? You will sign your name or it is no confession,
15 Mister! *(His breath heaving with agonized breathing, Proctor now lays the paper down and signs his name.)*

PARRIS: Praise be to the Lord!

(Proctor has just finished signing when
20 *Danforth reaches for the paper. But Proctor snatches it up, and now a wild terror is rising in him, and a boundless anger.)*

DANFORTH: *(perplexed, but politely extending his hand)* If you please, sir.
25

PROCTOR: No.

DANFORTH: *(as though Proctor did not understand)* Mr. Proctor, I must have—

PROCTOR: No, no. I have signed it. You
30 have seen me. It is done! You have no need for this.

PARRIS: Proctor, the village must have proof that—

PROCTOR: Damn the village! I confess to
35 God, and God has seen my name on this! It is enough!

DANFORTH: No, sir, it is—

PROCTOR: You came to save my soul, did you not? Here! I have confessed myself; it is enough!

40 DANFORTH: You have not con—

PROCTOR: I have confessed myself! Is there no good penitence but it be public? God does not need my name nailed upon the church! God sees my name; God
45 knows how black my sins really are! It is enough!

DANFORTH: Mr. Proctor—

PROCTOR: You will not use me! I am no Sarah Good or Tituba, I am John Proctor!
50 You will not use me! It is no part of salvation that you should use me!

DANFORTH: I do not wish to—

PROCTOR: I have three children—how may I teach them to walk like men in the
55 world, and I sold my friends?

DANFORTH: You have not sold your friends—

PROCTOR: Beguile me not! I blacken all of them when this is nailed to the church
60 the very day they hang for silence!

DANFORTH: Mr. Proctor, I must have good and legal proof that you—

PROCTOR: You are the high court, your word is good enough! Tell them I
65 confessed myself; say Proctor broke his knees and wept like a woman; say what you will, but my name cannot—

—Excerpted from *The Crucible* by Arthur Miller

49. What does Proctor mean when he says, "I blacken all of them when this is nailed to the church … !" (lines 58–60)?

(1) His confession will ruin his family's reputation in the village.

(2) Posting Proctor's false confession dishonors those who told the truth.

(3) Proctor is ashamed of his sins and will be embarrassed by the confession.

(4) He regrets how his confession will haunt his three children for their lives.

(5) Proctor has doomed his friends by his past actions and his confession.

50. Who could best identify with Proctor's situation?

(1) a prisoner of war

(2) a trial judge

(3) a military officer

(4) a police officer

(5) a hardened criminal

51. Which statement best summarizes Proctor's feelings throughout the passage?

(1) He is sorry for his offenses.

(2) He is angry with his friends.

(3) He fears dishonoring his name.

(4) He is afraid of his punishment.

(5) He doesn't trust the court.

52. Which word best describes the language of Danforth's dialogue?

(1) frustrated

(2) friendly

(3) regretful

(4) humble

(5) arrogant

53. What can you infer is Proctor's purpose for keeping the signed confession?

(1) He doesn't want his wife to see it.

(2) He fears what the townspeople will do.

(3) He thinks that the act of signing is sufficient.

(4) He is aware that he has signed his death order.

(5) He was not telling the truth in the confession.

54. The playwright was comparing the witch trials in this play and John Proctor's confession to government hearings in the 1950s which urged witnesses to betray their friends and colleagues.

Based on this information and the passage, whom do you infer the playwright intends John Proctor's character to represent?

A man who

(1) is forced to betray his country

(2) searches for his family's respect

(3) looks for a solution to his punishment

(4) wants to do the honorable thing

(5) sacrifices his friends for his own life

Answers are on pages 110–113.

Directions: The purpose of this practice test is to help you identify the skills you will need in order to be successful on the new 2002 GED Language Arts, Reading Test. This test consists of forty multiple-choice questions based on seven passages of fiction, nonfiction, poetry, and drama. You should take no longer than 65 minutes to complete this test.

After you read each passage, you will be asked questions to determine your understanding of what you've read. For example, you may be asked to make inferences, draw conclusions, or predict the outcome of the story. You may need to apply the ideas or information you've read to other situations. You may be given additional information to use in answering questions about the passage. Answer each question carefully and thoughtfully, choosing the best answer from the five choices. When you complete the test, check your work with the answers and explanations on pages 94–95.

Practice Test Answer Grid

1	① ② ③ ④ ⑤		15	① ② ③ ④ ⑤		29	① ② ③ ④ ⑤
2	① ② ③ ④ ⑤		16	① ② ③ ④ ⑤		30	① ② ③ ④ ⑤
3	① ② ③ ④ ⑤		17	① ② ③ ④ ⑤		31	① ② ③ ④ ⑤
4	① ② ③ ④ ⑤		18	① ② ③ ④ ⑤		32	① ② ③ ④ ⑤
5	① ② ③ ④ ⑤		19	① ② ③ ④ ⑤		33	① ② ③ ④ ⑤
6	① ② ③ ④ ⑤		20	① ② ③ ④ ⑤		34	① ② ③ ④ ⑤
7	① ② ③ ④ ⑤		21	① ② ③ ④ ⑤		35	① ② ③ ④ ⑤
8	① ② ③ ④ ⑤		22	① ② ③ ④ ⑤		36	① ② ③ ④ ⑤
9	① ② ③ ④ ⑤		23	① ② ③ ④ ⑤		37	① ② ③ ④ ⑤
10	① ② ③ ④ ⑤		24	① ② ③ ④ ⑤		38	① ② ③ ④ ⑤
11	① ② ③ ④ ⑤		25	① ② ③ ④ ⑤		39	① ② ③ ④ ⑤
12	① ② ③ ④ ⑤		26	① ② ③ ④ ⑤		40	① ② ③ ④ ⑤
13	① ② ③ ④ ⑤		27	① ② ③ ④ ⑤			
14	① ② ③ ④ ⑤		28	① ② ③ ④ ⑤			

Questions 1–6 refer to the following excerpt from a play.

HOW DO THESE MEN FEEL ABOUT EACH OTHER?

Act One

Scene: Lights come up on a cheap, ground-floor apartment on the outskirts of Cucamonga. A sign with this single place-name, "CUCAMONGA," hangs above the
5 *set. The apartment is very sparse. A sink piled with dirty dishes against the stage-right wall. A bed with one blanket against the left wall. A pile of dirty clothes at the foot of the bed, on the floor. Rough stucco*
10 *walls in pale green, absolutely bare with no attempt to decorate. A window in each wall trimmed in pale Mexican orange with sun-bleached plastic curtains. The windows look out into black space. No trees. No buildings.*
15 *No landscape of any kind. Just black.*

Actors have entered in the dark. Lights come up on VINNIE, sitting on the edge of the bed, elbows on knees, staring at the floor. He's dressed in a dark blue long-
20 *sleeved shirt, dark slacks with no belt. Everything very rumpled as though he's been sleeping in his clothes for weeks. Bare feet. CARTER peruses the room, crossing from one window to the next, looking out,*
25 *then moving to the sink. He's dressed in a very expensive beige suit, dark tie, brown overcoat slung over one arm and a briefcase containing his cellular phone. His shoes are alligator loafers with little tassels. Both men*
30 *are well into their forties.*

CARTER: Well, this isn't bad, Vinnie. Cozy. Close to the mall. Little sparse maybe. Picture I had was that you were much worse off.

35 VINNIE: What's sparse about it?

CARTER: Well—it could use a lady's touch. You know—a few throw-rugs or something. What do they call those? You know—throw-rugs.

40 VINNIE: All's I need is a bed.

CARTER: Sixties style, huh?

VINNIE: I didn't have a bed in the sixties.

Pause.

CARTER: Right. Well, you got someone
45 looking after you? Someone to do the laundry? Dishes? I can get that arranged for you if you want. Local talent.

VINNIE: I'm fine.

CARTER: Okay. *(Moves to pile of laundry.)*
50 But you shouldn't ought to let the laundry pile up on you, Vinnie. You let that happen, it starts to go sour. Gives you a bad impression of yourself.

VINNIE: I don't need the laundry for that.

55 *Pause.*

CARTER: You taking care of yourself otherwise? Not too much booze?

VINNIE: Not too much.

CARTER: Get out for a uh—stroll now and
60 then? Fresh air. Blood pumping?

VINNIE: I walk everywhere.

CARTER: Good! That's good. Gotta keep your health up. Funny how the mind follows the body. Ever noticed that?

—Excerpted from *Simpatico,*
by Sam Shephard 1995

1. What do Carter's clothes suggest about him?

   (1) He's successful.
   (2) He's creative and artistic.
   (3) He's been traveling a long time.
   (4) He doesn't care about appearances.
   (5) He has a lot in common with Vinnie.

2. What does the following dialogue suggest about Vinnie's character?

   CARTER: But you shouldn't ought to let the laundry pile up on you, Vinnie. You let that happen, it starts to go sour. Gives you a bad impression of yourself.

   VINNIE: I don't need the laundry for that.

   (1) Vinnie is very proud.
   (2) Vinnie isn't very smart.
   (3) Vinnie has a low opinion of himself.
   (4) Vinnie likes having a messy apartment.
   (5) Vinnie used to have a good job and a big house.

3. Which word best describes Carter's attitude toward Vinnie?

   (1) awestruck
   (2) resentful
   (3) protective
   (4) threatening
   (5) all-knowing

4. Which of the following statements best describes the advice that Carter gives Vinnie?

   (1) It's really intended to make life easier for Carter.
   (2) It's weak and doesn't address Vinnie's real problems.
   (3) It is aimed at tricking Vinnie and keeping him helpless.
   (4) It suggests that all of Vinnie's problems would disappear if he married.
   (5) It is insightful and shows that Carter has been thinking a lot about Vinnie.

5. What do Vinnie's words and actions suggest about his mood?

   (1) He is depressed.
   (2) He isn't letting Carter get to him.
   (3) He is touched that Carter came to visit.
   (4) He has something more important to do.
   (5) He has no idea what is going on around him.

6. The playwright, Sam Shepard, is known for weaving science fiction and mythical elements into his plays; for using clever humor and blunt dialogue; and for writing about the Old West. Which of these characteristics is most obvious in the passage you just read?

   (1) blunt dialogue
   (2) clever humor
   (3) science fiction
   (4) the Old West
   (5) references to myth

Questions 7–12 refer to the following excerpt from a short story.

WHAT DO THESE MEN THINK OF EACH OTHER?

Once upon a time I found a ten-cent magazine lying on a bench in a little city park. Anyhow, that was the amount he asked me for when I sat on the bench next
5   to him. He was a musty, dingy, and tattered magazine, with some queer stories bound in him, I was sure. He turned out to be a scrapbook.

"I am a newspaper reporter," I said to
10   him, to try him. "I have been detailed to write up some of the experiences of the unfortunate ones who spend their evenings in this park. May I ask you to what you attribute your downfall in—"

15   I was interrupted by a laugh from my purchase—a laugh so rusty and unpracticed that I was sure it had been his first for many a day.

"Oh, no, no," said he. "You ain't a
20   reporter. Reporters don't talk that way. They pretend to be one of us, and say they've just got on the blind baggage from St. Louis. I can tell a reporter on sight. Us park bums get to be fine judges of human nature. We
25   sit here all day and watch the people go by. I can size up anybody who walks past my bench in a way that would surprise you."

"Well," I said, "go on and tell me. How do you size me up?"

30   "I should say," said the student of human nature with unpardonable hesitation, "that you was, say, in the contracting business—or maybe worked in a store—or was a signpainter. You stopped in the park
35   to finish your cigar, and thought you'd get a little free monolog out of me. Still, you might be a plasterer or a lawyer—it's getting kind of dark, you see. And your wife won't let you smoke at home."

40   I frowned gloomily.

"But, judging again," went on the reader of men, "I'd say you ain't got a wife."

"No," said I, rising restlessly. "No, no, no, I ain't. But I *will* have, by the arrows of
45   Cupid. That is if—" My voice must have trailed away and muffled itself in uncertainty and despair.

"I see you have a story yourself," said the dusty vagrant—imprudently, it seemed
50   to me. "Suppose you take your dime back and spin your yarn for me. I'm interested myself in the ups and downs of unfortunate ones who spend their evenings in the park."

—Excerpted from "The Higher Pragmatism"
by O. Henry, in *Options*, 1909

7. What problem does the narrator admit to having?

    (1) He is homeless.
    (2) He lost his job.
    (3) He hates his boss.
    (4) He's unlucky in love.
    (5) He can't stop smoking.

8. Why does the narrator compare the man on the bench to a magazine?

    (1) He knows the man works for a magazine.
    (2) He is impressed by the man's ability to "read" people.
    (3) He thinks the man's face looks like a picture in a magazine.
    (4) He notices that the man's speech sounds like the writing in a magazine.
    (5) He hopes the man will tell entertaining stories, like those in magazines.

9. Which of the following best describes the narrator's writing style?

    (1) brief and to-the-point
    (2) unemotional and not very descriptive
    (3) careful and formal, except when he's upset
    (4) casual, like speech you might hear on the street
    (5) wild and uncensored, expressing anything that comes to mind

10. If the author were to read this story aloud, what tone of voice would he probably use?

    (1) angry
    (2) amused
    (3) dazzled
    (4) shocked
    (5) disappointed

11. Which of the following literary techniques does the author use to make the ending of this passage more effective?

    (1) an ironic or unexpected turn of events
    (2) rising suspense over what will happen in the end
    (3) statement of a strong moral drawn from events in the story
    (4) evidence that the narrator has changed over the course of the story
    (5) anachronism, or something that doesn't belong in the time when the story is set

12. What does the vagrant think makes him such a good judge of people?

    (1) He is old and wise.
    (2) He is naturally intelligent.
    (3) He watches people all day.
    (4) He has had a lot of hard times.
    (5) He meets many foolish people.

Questions 13–18 refer to the following poem.

HOW HAS THE SPEAKER GROWN AND CHANGED?

The River-Merchant's Wife: A Letter

While my hair was still cut straight across my forehead
Played I about the front gate, pulling flowers.
You came by on bamboo stilts, playing horse,
You walked about my seat, playing with blue plums.
5 And we went on living in the village of Chokan:
Two small people, without dislike or suspicion.

At fourteen I married My Lord you.
I never laughed, being bashful.
Lowering my head, I looked at the wall.
10 Called to, a thousand times, I never looked back.

At fifteen I stopped scowling,
I desired my dust to be mingled with yours
Forever and forever and forever.
Why should I climb the look out?

15 At sixteen you departed,
You went into far Ku-to-yen, by the river of swirling eddies,
And you have been gone five months.
The monkeys make sorrowful noise overhead.

You dragged your feet when you went out.
20 By the gate now, the moss is grown, the
different mosses,
Too deep to clear them away!
The leaves fall early this autumn, in wind.
The paired butterflies are already yellow with August
25 Over the grass in the West garden;
They hurt me. I grow older.

If you are coming down through the narrows
of the river Kiang,
Please let me know beforehand,
30 And I will come out to meet you
As far as Cho-fu-Sa.

—Ezra Pound, from Cathay: *Translations,* 1915

13. At the time she writes, how does the speaker feel about her husband?

   (1) She is afraid of him.
   (2) She loves him intensely.
   (3) She has always admired him.
   (4) She is disappointed in him.
   (5) She accepts him in spite of his faults.

14. The poet uses moss by the garden gate (lines 20–21) to illustrate what point about the speaker?

   (1) She is a bad housekeeper.
   (2) She loves growing things.
   (3) She lives in a wet climate.
   (4) She lives in an old house.
   (5) She doesn't see many people.

15. When she says, "I desired my dust to be mingled with yours/Forever and forever and forever" (lines 12–13), what does the speaker want?

   (1) to marry her future husband
   (2) to be buried with her husband
   (3) to be reunited with her husband
   (4) to have children with her husband
   (5) to live in the same house as her husband

16. According to the organization of this poem, what is discussed in each stanza?

   (1) season of the year
   (2) point in the cycle of life and death
   (3) aspect of the speaker's personality
   (4) reason the speaker misses her husband
   (5) stage in the speaker's relationship with her husband

17. The speaker's description of herself at fifteen suggests that if someone had asked her to go to Cho-fu-Sa then, what would her answer have been?

   (1) I can't go. I'm too young.
   (2) Why should I? I'm happy here.
   (3) Oh, yes. I'm longing for adventure!
   (4) I'd love to get away from this house.
   (5) I'll come as long as my husband stays at home.

18. How do the paired butterflies "hurt" the speaker (lines 24–26)?

   (1) by eating her plants
   (2) by dying before her eyes
   (3) by making her feel ugly in comparison
   (4) by flying away and leaving her behind
   (5) by reminding her that she isn't with her mate

Questions 19–24 refer to the following excerpt from a short story.

HOW DOES MAGGIE FEEL ABOUT HER RELATIVES?

Maggie had not intended to get sucked in on this thing, sleeping straight through the christening, steering clear of the punch bowl, and refusing to dress for
5 company. But when she glanced over my grandfather's shoulder and saw "Aspire, Enspire, Perspire" scrawled across the first page in that hard-core Protestant hand, and a grease stain from the fried chicken too,
10 something snapped in her head. She snatched up the book and retired rapidly to her room, locked my mother out, and explained through the door that my mother was a fool to encourage a lot of misspelled
15 nonsense from Mr. Tyler's kin, and an even bigger fool for having married the monster in the first place.

I imagine that Maggie sat at her great oak desk, rolled the lace cuffs gently back,
20 and dipped her quill into the lavender ink pot with all the ceremony due the Emancipation Proclamation, which was, after all, exactly what she was drafting. Writing to me, she explained, was serious business, for
25 she felt called upon to liberate me from all historical and genealogical connections except the most divine. In short, the family was a disgrace, degrading Maggie's and my capacity for wings, as they say. I can only say
30 that Maggie was truly inspired. And she probably ruined my life from the get-go.

There is a photo of the two of us on the second page. There's Maggie in Minnie Mouse shoes and a long polka-dot affair
35 with her stockings rolled up at the shins, looking like muffins. There's me with nothing much at all on, in her arms, and looking almost like a normal, mortal, everyday-type baby—raw, wrinkled, ugly. Except that it
40 must be clearly understood straightaway that I sprang into the world full wise and invulnerable and gorgeous like a goddess.

—Toni Cade Bambara, excerpted from "Maggie of the Green Bottles" in *Gorilla, My Love,* 1960

19. Which word best describes Maggie's personality?

(1) warm
(2) timid
(3) odd
(4) polite
(5) charming

20. In the line "Maggie had not intended to get sucked in on this thing" (lines 1–2), what is "this thing"?

(1) this story
(2) the narrator's family
(3) oversleeping, laziness
(4) celebration of the narrator's birth
(5) an obsession with parties and good times

21. What is the main thing Maggie tried to do for her niece when she wrote in the baby book?

(1) give her faith in God
(2) make her proud of her family
(3) make her feel free to be herself
(4) persuade her to run away from home
(5) give her information about her family history

22. What bothered Maggie about the comment the grandfather wrote in the narrator's baby book?

(1) It was too common and confining.
(2) It was too bossy.
(3) It criticized Maggie.
(4) It assumed that the baby was stupid.
(5) It was advice the grandfather didn't follow himself.

23. Which of the following articles of clothing would Maggie be most likely to wear?

(1) nurse's shoes
(2) an old, stained dress
(3) overalls and a flannel shirt
(4) a nylon jogging suit in bright colors
(5) an old-fashioned hat covered with silk flowers

24. The final line of this passage suggests that the narrator reacted in what way to the message Maggie wrote in her baby book?

(1) She ignored it.
(2) She believed it.
(3) She thought it was funny.
(4) She thought it was ridiculous.
(5) She thought Maggie was flattering herself.

Questions 25–29 refer to the following excerpt from a nonfiction article.

WHAT IS THE WRITER'S TONE IN THIS PASSAGE?

We live in an age of media consultants and "handlers" who choreograph a politician's every move. Whatever a politician's biography and beliefs, it often
5 seems that what matters most now is not actual experiences or ideas, but the ability to communicate a convincing image. Acting presidential is one thing, appearing presidential can be another, and in the
10 contemporary United States, it is hard to know which is more important.

In America, the first president to exploit photography was not Teddy Roosevelt, or Franklin Delano Roosevelt, or
15 John Kennedy, though all were masters of photographic presentation, whether on the campaign trail or sitting in the Oval Office. It was Abraham Lincoln, whose election was aided by a Mathew Brady photograph,
20 widely reproduced (in woodcut form as well as photographic prints) that made him appear more handsome and less gangly. Brady pulled up Lincoln's collar to cover his long neck, retouched his face to eliminate
25 the gauntness, and in general gave him what we would now call a photographic make-over. From that day to this, presidents have struggled to look good, with official photographers hired by the White House,
30 and a running battle to control the press at all points even with their telephoto lenses and general sneakiness and "get the picture or die" attitude.

Nothing is so rare these days as real
35 spontaneity, not the planned media events that include even the calculated casualness of a walk on the beach. "Photo-ops" (i.e., "photographic opportunities") are carefully staged rituals, with each photographer
40 making a nearly identical version of the same picture. Looking through a newspaper or weekly magazine, it is hard to find a photograph of a politician that does not appear staged—although those exceptions
45 are still worth looking for. Far more common, however, are the endless variations on the same basic image, or copies of previous favorites. What might once have been spontaneous—JFK with his
50 children—becomes the model to be copied by later officeholders.

—Excerpted from *American Photography: A Century of Images*, by KTCA in association with Middlemarch Films, 1999

25. Which of the following does the writer most probably try to ignore when he or she decides how to vote?

(1) whether the candidates have previously held office
(2) whether he or she agrees with the candidate's views on issues
(3) whether the candidates make their points with style
(4) whether the candidates have made major mistakes in the past
(5) whether the actions candidates plan to take will really improve government

26. Based on this passage, which of the following photographs would the writer find most interesting?

(1) a surprise photo of the president taken by his sister
(2) a photograph of the president posing with his children
(3) the president's photograph taken for the White House portrait gallery
(4) an official White House photograph of the president and the first lady
(5) a newspaper photograph of the president signing an important treaty

27. The author describes Abraham Lincoln's portrait as an example of which of the following?

(1) a president who really didn't care how he looked
(2) how manipulation of photographs has changed over time
(3) the first photograph altered to make a president look better
(4) how "photographic makeovers" can actually make a president look worse
(5) the way photographs were taken before "handlers" choreographed a president's every move

28. Which statement best expresses the author's opinion of photographers with a "get the picture or die" attitude (lines 32–33)?

(1) He thinks they are destroying American news.
(2) He applauds them for their creativity and spunk.
(3) He blames them for the lack of spontaneity in presidential photographs.
(4) He doesn't like their tactics but is glad they try to take unofficial photos.
(5) He believes that one day they will overcome the power of presidential handlers.

29. Which of the following statements from the passage is a fact?

(1) "it often seems that what matters most now is not actual experiences or ideas" (lines 4–6)
(2) "in the contemporary United States, it is hard to know which is more important, [acting presidential, or appearing presidential]" (lines 9–11)
(3) "all [presidents T. Roosevelt, F. Roosevelt, and Kennedy] were masters of photographic presentation" (lines 15–16)
(4) "Brady pulled up Lincoln's collar . . . [and] retouched his face" (lines 23–24)
(5) "Nothing is so rare these days as real spontaneity" (lines 34–35)

Questions 30–35 refer to the following excerpt from a short story.

WHAT KIND OF FAMILY IS THIS?

So the first thing Stella-Rondo did at the table was turn Papa-Daddy against me.

"Papa-Daddy," she says. He was trying to cut up his meat. "Papa-Daddy!" I was
5 taken completely by surprise. Papa-Daddy is about a million years old and's got this long-long beard. "Papa-Daddy, Sister says she fails to understand why you don't cut off your beard."

10 So Papa-Daddy l-a-y-s down his knife and fork! He's real rich. Mama says he is, he says he isn't. So he says, "Have I heard correctly? You don't understand why I don't cut off my beard?"

15 "Why," I says, "Papa-Daddy, of course I understand, I did not say any such of a thing, the idea!"

He says, "Hussy!"

I says, "Papa-Daddy, you know I
20 wouldn't any more want you to cut off your beard than the man in the moon. It was the farthest thing from my mind! Stella-Rondo sat there and made that up while she was eating breast of chicken."

25 But he says, "So the postmistress fails to understand why I don't cut off my beard. Which job I got you through my influence with the government. 'Bird's nest'—is that what you call it?"

30 Not that it isn't the next to smallest P.O. in the entire state of Mississippi.

I says, "Oh, Papa-Daddy," I says, "I didn't say any such of a thing, I never dreamed it was a bird's nest, I have always
35 been grateful though this is the next to smallest P.O. in the state of Mississippi, and I do not enjoy being referred to as a hussy by my own grandfather."

But Stella-Rondo says, "Yes, you did
40 say it too. Anybody in the world could of heard you, that had ears."

"Stop right there," says Mama, looking at me.

So I pulled my napkin straight back
45 through the napkin ring and left the table.

As soon as I was out of the room Mama says, "Call her back, or she'll starve to death," but Papa-Daddy says, "This is the beard I started growing on the Coast when I
50 was fifteen years old." He would of gone on till nightfall if Shirley-T. hadn't lost the Milky Way she ate in Cairo.

So Papa-Daddy says, "I am going out and lie in the hammock, and you can all sit
55 here and remember my words: I'll never cut off my beard as long as I live, even one inch, and I don't appreciate it in you at all." Passed right by me in the hall and went straight out and got in the hammock.

—Excerpted from "Why I Live at the P.O."
by Eudora Welty, in *A Curtain of Green and
Other Stories*, 1941

30. Why does the narrator leave the dinner table?

  (1) Mama sends her to her room.
  (2) Shirley-T. loses her candy bar.
  (3) She has to admit that she's guilty.
  (4) She can't think of anything more to say.
  (5) She realizes that no one is going to support her.

31. Which of the following is a trait of the narrator's writing style in this passage?

  (1) big words
  (2) misspellings
  (3) unusual settings
  (4) irrelevant details
  (5) sudden changes in time

32. In paragraph 3, why does the narrator separate the letters in the word *lays* with hyphens?

  (1) to demonstrate that she knows how to spell *lays*
  (2) to point out that she is using the correct form of *lays*
  (3) to let us know that *lays* is an unusual word for her to use
  (4) to show that Papa-Daddy laid down his knife and fork very slowly
  (5) to indicate that she didn't let other people at the table know what she was saying

33. What does the author want readers to think of this narrator?

  (1) She's lying.
  (2) She's selfish.
  (3) She's funny.
  (4) She's abused.
  (5) She's spoiled.

34. Which of the following sentences most nearly matches the narrator's style?

  (1) Every Fourth of July we get together. You can bet on it.
  (2) So my family. There are nine of us. We get together every Fourth of July sure as shootin.
  (3) Our family, we meet on the Fourth of July, our favorite holiday, nearly every single year.
  (4) For us, the Fourth of July is like a family album. We use it to remember each other and our past.
  (5) On hot, muggy, Fourth-of-July week-ends, we tell old family stories, eat cold potato salad, and play fierce games of Scrabble long into the night.

35. Why does Papa-Daddy expect special treatment from the narrator?

  (1) She's his favorite.
  (2) He got her a job.
  (3) He knows her secrets.
  (4) She's his only granddaughter.
  (5) She's always been the "good" granddaughter.

Questions 36–40 refer to the following excerpt from an autobiography.

HOW DOES THE AUTHOR SEE HIMSELF?

I have taken Caliban's advice. I have stolen their books. I will have some run of this isle.

Once upon a time, I was a 'socially
5   disadvantaged' child. An enchantedly happy child. Mine was a childhood of intense family closeness. And extreme public alienation.

Thirty years later I write this book as a middle-class American man. Assimilated
10 [adopted into another culture].

Dark-skinned. To be seen at a Belgravia dinner party. Or in New York. Exotic in a tuxedo. My face is drawn to severe Indian features which would pass
15 notice on the page of a National Geographic, but at a cocktail party in Bel Air somebody wonders: 'Have you ever thought of doing any high-fashion modeling? Take this card.' (In Beverly Hills will this monster
20 make a man.)

A lady in a green dress asks, 'Didn't we meet at the Thompsons' party last month in Malibu?'

And, 'What do you do, Mr. Rodriguez?'

25 I write: I am a writer.

A part-time writer. When I began this book, five years ago, a fellowship bought me a year of continuous silence in my San Francisco apartment. But the words
30 wouldn't come. The money ran out. So I was forced to take temporary jobs. (I have friends who, with a phone call, can find me well-paying work.) In past months I have found myself in New York. In Los Angeles.
35 Working. With money. Among people with money. And at leisure—a weekend guest in Connecticut; at a cocktail party in Bel Air.

Perhaps because I have always, accidentally, been a classmate to children of
40 rich parents, I long ago came to assume my association with their world; came to assume that I could have money, if it was money I

wanted. But money, big money, has never been the goal of my life. My story is not a
45 version of Sammy Glick's [an immoral movie producer in a novel]. I work to support my habit of writing. The great luxury of my life is the freedom to sit at this desk.

—Excerpted from *Hunger of Memory*,
by Richard Rodriguez, 1982

36. Caliban (line 1) is a primitive man in Shakespeare's play *The Tempest*. An Italian duke teaches Caliban to speak but steals Caliban's island. In what way is the writer like Caliban?

   (1) He loves Shakespeare.
   (2) He, too, lives on an island.
   (3) He stole a book from the library once, and Caliban was a thief.
   (4) He is different from the people around him and has adopted their ways.
   (5) He jogs, and that makes him feel like Caliban running around on his island.

37. Into what kind of series is the information in paragraphs two and four organized?

   (1) exaggerations
   (2) rich descriptions
   (3) emotional stories
   (4) quotes from well-known experts
   (5) apparent opposites or contradictions

38. How does the author feel when he is at parties in Bel Air and Belgravia (paragraph 4)?

   (1) lucky
   (2) out-of-place
   (3) very American
   (4) relaxed and at ease
   (5) superior to those around him

39. Which of the following words best describes the author's lifestyle?

   (1) cozy
   (2) boring
   (3) simple
   (4) privileged
   (5) back breaking

40. When the author says "a fellowship bought me a year of continuous silence in my San Francisco apartment" (lines 27–29), what does he mean?

   (1) He was paid to stop writing.
   (2) He was paid to mind his own business.
   (3) He was given money to stay home and write.
   (4) He paid his neighbors to keep quiet so he could concentrate.
   (5) He was given enough money so that he didn't have to write for a year.

Answer Key

1. (1) Carter wears "a very expensive beige suit," so he must make a lot of money.

2. (3) Vinnie is saying that he has a bad impression of himself even without the laundry.

3. (3) Carter tries to protect Vinnie from bad health, bad housekeeping, and alcohol.

4. (2) Carter's advice is about small things (housekeeping and walks), while the descriptions of Vinnie and his apartment suggest that he has big problems.

5. (1) Vinnie stares at the floor, speaks little, and doesn't care for himself. All are signs of depression.

6. (1) Both characters speak in short sentences or fragments with very little description.

7. (4) The narrator admits, "No, no, no, I ain't [got a wife]. But I will have, by the arrows of Cupid. That is if—" His sputtering suggests that he is upset.

8. (5) The narrator guesses that the vagrant has "some queer stories bound in him," and he asks to hear the vagrant's story.

9. (3) The narrator uses perfect grammar and sophisticated vocabulary except when he's upset about not being married.

10. (2) The vagrant's odd manner and the way he turns the situation around on the narrator are meant to be funny.

11. (1) The narrator and vagrant switch positions. At first, the narrator offers the vagrant a dime in exchange for stories. In the end, the vagrant makes the same offer to him.

12. (3) The vagrant says, "Us park bums get to be fine judges of human nature. We sit here all day and watch the people go by."

13. (2) In the last stanza, the speaker expresses deep longing for her husband.

14. (5) The moss couldn't have grown so deep if people were walking through the gate to visit the speaker.

15. (2) Her body would turn to dust only after death, and then her dust could be mixed (mingled) with her husband's forever.

16. (5) In stanza 1 they meet, in stanza 2 they marry, in stanza 3 they fall in love, in stanza 4 they part. Stanza 5 is the present.

17. (2) At 15 she had no desire to leave home to climb the look out. Likewise, she would probably have had no desire to go to Cho-fu-Sa.

18. (5) The paired butterflies have their mates. Seeing them must remind her that her mate is far away.

19. (3) She wears Minnie Mouse clothes, gets upset over a misspelled word, and claims to be different from the rest of her family. All of this suggests that she is odd.

20. (4) The christening, the punch bowl, and the baby book all tell you that the family is celebrating the baby's birth.

21. (3) Maggie was "liberating" (or freeing) her because the family kept her from her "capacity for wings."

22. (1) The problem was that grandfather misspelled inspire, and he left chicken grease in the book. Both mistakes portrayed him as a common person. The message confined her in an ordinary life instead of liberating her as Maggie wished.

23. (5) The passage describes Maggie wearing old-fashioned, feminine clothes, like lace cuffs, polka dot dresses, and stockings rolled down around the shins.

24. (3) The tone of the entire passage is humorous. In the second paragraph, the narrator says that Maggie, with her comments, "probably ruined my life from the get-go." The final line appears to be exaggerated, implying that the narrator found Maggie's comments to be humorous.

25. (3) Style is a matter of appearances, and this writer thinks we should focus more on actions than on appearances.

26. (1) This photo would be more spontaneous or unplanned than the others.

27. (3) The writer says, "the first president to exploit photography was … Abraham Lincoln … [Brady] gave him what we would now call a photographic make-over."

28. (4) The writer's overall message is that official photos are bad. Nevertheless, the negative language in this quote suggests that he disapproves of "get the picture or die" tactics.

29. (4) One can't argue about whether Brady pulled up the collar and retouched Lincoln's face; it's simply a fact.

30. (5) She leaves the table right after Mama looks at her in a way that shows even Mama thinks she's lying.

31. (4) Papa-Daddy's money, the breast of chicken, the size of the P.O., the napkin ring, and Cairo are all details that have nothing to do with the real story.

32. (4) The narrator uses hyphens to stretch out the word lays, much as Papa stretched out the action of laying down his silverware.

33. (3) Most people would be amused by the narrator's peculiar speech habits and the absurd situation she describes.

34. (2) The narrator tends to interrupt her speech with short statements, like "There are nine of us," and she tends to use cliches such as "sure as shootin'."

35. (2) Papa-Daddy is especially angry at her criticism of his beard because he got her a job. He says, "Which job [postmistress] I got you through my influence with the government."

36. (4) The author describes how he is different from the white-skinned people around him and how he has assimilated their language and culture.

37. (5) "Socially disadvantaged" seems the opposite of "enchantedly happy," "closeness" is the opposite of "alienation," and the writer's "Indian features" are contrasted with the environment at Belgravia dinner parties.

38. (2) The author stresses how he, with his dark skin, doesn't fit in at those parties.

39. (4) The author says, "I have found myself in New York. In Los Angeles. Working. With money. Among people with money. And at leisure …"

40. (3) The author began this book during that year, so he must have been writing.

Evaluation Chart

Use the chart below to identify the reading content areas and skill areas you need to review before you take the 2002 GED Language Arts, Reading Test. Circle the number of any question you answered incorrectly. Then find the pages in each book that will help you review the material.

The reading skills listed across the top of the chart are absolutely essential for success on the test. If you got several items wrong in a column, you should review that reading skill in Contemporary's *GED Language Arts, Reading* or *Complete GED*.

Skill Area/Content Area	Comprehension (R*: 15–37) (C*: 217–230)	Application (R: 39–46) (C: 231–236)	Analysis (R: 47–88) (C: 237–262)	Synthesis (R: 89–105) (C: 263–270)
Nonfiction Prose (R: 109–164) (C: 655–684)	27, 40	25, 26	29, 38, 39	28, 36, 37
Prose Fiction (R: 165–215) (C: 589–614)	7, 12, 20, 21, 35	10, 23	8, 11, 19, 22 24, 30, 32	9, 30, 31, 33 34
Poetry (R: 217–247) (C: 615–636)	13, 15	17	14, 16, 18	
Drama (R: 249–281) (C: 637–654)			1, 2	3, 4, 5, 6

* R=Contemporary's *GED Language Arts, Reading*
  C=Contemporary's *Complete GED*

Answer Key

Nonfiction Prose

Informational Nonfiction, pages 3–17

1. **(3) Comprehension/Supporting Details**
   Since the author states that arson means "deliberately setting something afire" (line 13), you can conclude that an arsonist is a person who intentionally burns property.

2. **(4) Comprehension/Main Idea**
   This sentence, directly stated in lines 6–7, summarizes the major point of the passage. The other statements are all supporting details mentioned later in the passage.

3. **(2) Comprehension/Supporting Details**
   Lines 1–2 state, "The laws of each state determine what is considered a crime."

4. **(5) Analysis/Structure**
   The introductory sentence of the second paragraph states that there are "two kinds of crimes." Lines 25–27 state, "Crimes may also be classified as being against persons or against property." These two sentences explain how the information is structured.

5. **(2) Application**
   Shoplifting is a misdemeanor because it is not generally considered a serious crime.

6. **(2) Comprehension/Main Idea**
   The introductory sentence states that many of the issues receiving media attention are family issues. The author later states that the focus of her discussion is the importance of the family environment. The other choices are all supporting details that comment on this central issue.

7. **(4) Comprehension/Supporting Details**
   Lines 28–29 state that "parents rightfully bear the primary responsibility for children in this society."

8. **(1) Application**
   The author believes that children need "supportive adult care" (line 20) and that "attitudes of the workplace ... profoundly affect the extent to which parents can provide their children with a good start" (lines 31–36). Therefore, the author would probably not support the firing of employees who occasionally stay home to care for young children.

9. **(4) Analysis/Supporting Details**
   Lines 20–21 state, "Children without supportive adult care are likely to lack confidence." A responsible, understanding father is a supportive adult. Therefore, you can logically conclude that he can increase his child's self-esteem.

10. **(2) Synthesis/Organization**
    The author analyzes the topic by giving examples of cause-and-effect relationships. Paragraphs 3, 4, and 5 each identify a situation (a cause) and its outcome (the effect).

11. **(3) Analysis/Figurative Language**
    The author is using the phrase "sudden death" figuratively. In the first paragraph the author further explains this image: "failure came suddenly and in a very frightening way" and "the feeling of utter defeat."

12. **(4) Application**
    Because engineers use what they know about science and mathematics to make useful structures and machines, they require extensive mathematical training.

13. **(4) Comprehension/Main Idea**
    The author states in lines 22–24, "A common myth about the nature of mathematical ability holds that one either has or does not have a mathematical mind." The author questions the validity of the notion that only people born with "mathematical minds" excel in this subject.

14. **(5) Comprehension/Supporting Details**
    The author states that instead of "asking questions" (the best approach to solving a new math problem), most students become anxious.

15. **(1) Synthesis/Organization**
    In the passage the author analyzes the problem of math-anxious students. She explains the causes and effects of math anxiety and discusses misconceptions about mathematical ability.

16. **(1) Comprehension/Main Idea**
    In lines 9–12, Lincoln directly states the main reason for delivering the speech: "We have come to dedicate a portion of that field as a final resting place for those who here gave their lives that that nation might live." In other words, he is paying tribute to "these honored dead" (line 27).

17. **(4) Analysis/Figurative Language**
    Lincoln is using the phrase figuratively, not literally. Lincoln is dedicating a portion of the battlefield as a cemetery, or "final resting place," for the soldiers who were killed at Gettysburg.

18. **(3) Synthesis/Main Idea**
    Lincoln concludes the speech with his political goal: "that government of the people, by the people, for the people, shall not perish from the earth" (lines 33–35). Lincoln defines democracy and states that his goal is for this political system to last forever.

19. **(2) Analysis/Style**
    Throughout the speech, Lincoln uses the personal pronouns *we* and *us* to show that he is speaking on behalf of all Americans who support the North. His reaction to the war dead is a heartfelt sense of loss. Therefore, "impersonal" does not accurately describe the writing style of the speech.

20. **(2) Extended Synthesis**
    Although Lincoln's speech was brief, it captured the essential point of the occasion—to honor those who gave their lives in defense of their cause. Lincoln's brief points used language that made an impression on the listeners so that they could carry his words away from the ceremony.

21. **(3) Comprehension/Main Idea**
    In the last sentence of the first paragraph, the author directly states the main topic of his speech: "prison camps" and "what an American prisoner of war lives through."

22. **(2) Analysis/Supporting Details**
    Because Major Rowe spent over five years as a prisoner of the Viet Cong, you can conclude that his first-hand experience makes him an authority on the subject.

23. **(5) Comprehension/Supporting Details**
    Lines 29–30 state that Major Rowe escaped in December 1968.

24. **(1) Synthesis/Tone**
    Major Rowe directly states both his purpose and background. The tone of the speech is straightforward because of his direct style in presenting information.

25. **(2) Application**
    The ordeal of hostage victims is most similar to the grueling experience of war prisoners.

26. **(2) Comprehension/Supporting Details**
    Lines 1–2 state, "To the Europeans, the rhythms and melodies of Indian music were unfamiliar."

27. **(1) Application**
    Indians "sang to their spirits—asking for help or giving thanks" (lines 10–12). Indians also believed that songs "were considered holy" (line 32). Prayers share these same characteristics.

28. **(5) Comprehension/Main Idea**
    The main idea is directly stated in the introductory sentence of the paragraph. The remaining supporting details develop this central point.

29. **(4) Analysis/Main Idea**
    The passage emphasizes that the Indians' music was an integral part of their religion and culture. The music was not intended to entertain audiences. Therefore, you can conclude that Indian music was not commercial.

30. **(3) Synthesis/Main Idea**
    The author's main purpose is to educate the reader. He presents information about Indian music and its cultural significance.

31. **(4) Analysis/Style**
    Images of destruction appear throughout the passage. Examples of descriptive language include "wiped out" (line 14) sections of the city, "debris of fallen walls" (lines 38–39), and "twisted" (line 39) steel rails.

32. **(3) Analysis/Figurative Language**

    Lines 21–22 states that "the smoke of San Francisco's burnings was a lurid tower." The phrase "lurid tower" is used figuratively to show the horror and the appearance of the smoke.

33. **(1) Comprehension/Supporting Details**

    In the last sentence of the passage the author describes the time span of the earthquake itself as "thirty seconds' twitching of the earth's crust."

34. **(2) Application**

    Bombings are man-made disasters.

35. **(5) Analysis/Main Idea**

    While all of the choices mentioned were affected by the earthquake, the author of this passage focuses on the effects of the earthquake on property. Examples of property damage include factories, warehouses, hotels, water mains, streets, and telephone and telegraph systems.

36. **(5) Extended Synthesis**

    In the author's later account of the earthquake he describes the people fleeing the disaster as "gracious" and courteous. Instead of panic, the people considered the devastation they all faced and behaved "with grace."

37. **(3) Comprehension/Supporting Details**

    Lines 1–2 describe Lynn Swann as "the great wide receiver of the Pittsburgh Steelers," a football team. Therefore, you can conclude that he was a football player.

38. **(2) Comprehension/Supporting Details**

    Lynn Swann doesn't include culture among the list of attributes required in sports.

39. **(3) Synthesis/Interpreting Purpose**

    Using the comparison and contrast method, Lynn Swann focuses on the relationship between dance and sports: "One can always see the presence of dance in sports" (lines 12–13). By serving on the Pittsburgh Ballet Theater's board of directors, he hopes that both football fans and ballet fans "will discover the similarities between two great activities" (lines 32–33).

40. **(4) Application**

    Jumps are one of ballet's most common steps. Therefore, a basketball player springing in the air would most closely resemble a ballet dancer performing a leap.

41. **(5) Analysis/Supporting Details**

    Lynn Swann states in lines 8–11, "Some of our greatest athletes might well have become some of our greatest dancers if prejudice against dancing for men had not stood in the way." As used in this context, "prejudice" refers to the attitudes stereotyping male dancers as unmasculine.

42. **(3) Application**

    Diversity brings "innovative and fresh new ideas" that would help in developing new products for the consuming public.

43. **(5) Comprehension/Supporting Details**

    The second paragraph states, "Today's corporations are built around groups."

44. **(4) Comprehension/Main Idea**

    According to the passage, diversity is more than just racial, gender, or educational differences; diversity includes a broad array of backgrounds.

45. **(2) Analysis/Main Idea**

    The passage states that today's problems require "out-of-the-ordinary" (lines 13–14) and innovative input from diverse groups.

46. **(5) Extended Synthesis**

    The communications company is looking to planning for the future and would need to seek input from various components of the communications field: technology, financial, legal, cost factors, market analysis.

47. **(2) Analysis/Main Idea**

    Approval of this leave form would ensure that the employee could return to the job following the approved leave period.

48. **(1) Comprehension/Supporting Details**

    The first paragraph of the form states that the employee should submit the form to his or her supervisor "at least 30 days before the leave is to commence, when practicable."

49. **(4) Comprehension/Supporting Details**

    The eligibility section of the form begins by determining whether the employee's length of employment qualifies him or her for leave.

50. **(2) Analysis/Supporting Details**

    The last section of the form requires the employee's signature agreeing to return to work following the approved leave period.

51. **(3) Comprehension**

The passage discusses an employee's right to return to his or her job at the conclusion of a jury duty assignment.

52. **(1) Analysis/Supporting Details**

The third paragraph states, "A handful of states require employers to pay employees while on jury duty." The employee needs to check with the court to see if the state has that requirement.

53. **(2) Comprehension/Supporting Details**

The job protection issue of the law protects "permanent employees." The second paragraph states that the law does not require employers to pay "nonexempt salaried or hourly employees," but that "exempt employees who are absent from work to perform jury service must be paid their full salaries."

54. **(4) Analysis/Supporting Detail**

The survey reports that 90% of employers nationwide offer paid leave for jury duty.

Literary Nonfiction, pages 18–27

1. **(4) Comprehension/Supporting Details**

The phrase following *boondocker*, "the boy from the back country" (lines 5–6), explains the meaning of boondocker. The back country refers to a rural area.

2. **(5) Comprehension/Supporting Details**

Line 11 states, "Yeager grew up in Hamlin, West Virginia."

3. **(1) Comprehension/Supporting Details**

The last sentence in the passage states, "What was puzzling was the way Yeager talked."

4. **(2) Synthesis/Main Idea**

The supporting details in the passage discuss Yeager's personality, behavior, career, and upbringing.

5. **(3) Analysis/Style**

By describing Yeager's change of clothes, the author vividly illustrates Yeager's transition from a civilian in a rural environment to a pilot in the military.

6. **(5) Application**

You can assume that courage is a determining factor in a pilot's success. For example, Yeager proved his courage as a World War II pilot, yet he was not sophisticated, well educated, wealthy, or articulate.

7. **(3) Extended Synthesis**

Yeager's experiences with flight began in 1943. His lack of physical stature concealed his courageous exploits. He had the "right stuff" and was a model for the Mercury astronauts.

8. **(3) Analysis/Style**

The sports announcer's broadcast is a technique that the author uses to present a lively, first-hand account of the fight. As a result, the reader experiences an immediate sense of the action.

9. **(1) Comprehension/Supporting Details**

Lines 22 and 39 mention "the store," the place where the people are listening to the fight.

10. **(4) Analysis/Supporting Details**

Lines 3–4 state "There was no time to be relieved. The worst might still happen." Therefore, you can conclude that the author feels anxious.

11. **(5) Synthesis/Interpreting Purpose**

In lines 34–36, the author states, "Champion of the world. A Black boy. Some Black mother's son. He was the strongest man in the world." These sentences portray Joe Louis as a heroic figure in black history.

12. **(4) Application**

Because film consists of a continuous series of visual images, a filmmaker would most effectively portray the nonstop action of a prizefight. A photographer, a cartoonist, a sculptor, and a painter would be able to depict only isolated poses.

13. **(1) Extended Synthesis**

It was very important to the people listening that Joe Louis win. They were "holding themselves in against tremendous pressure" because they didn't want to get their hopes up too soon.

14. **(2) Comprehension/Main Idea**
    The supporting details of the passage develop the topic of medical practices during the author's childhood. The author lists examples of commonly used medicines and methods for treating the sick.

15. **(5) Analysis/Structure**
    This colorful example of childhood injuries is an effective introduction to the rest of the paragraph, which describes other instances that needed medical attention.

16. **(3) Comprehension/Supporting Details**
    The author directly states in lines 35–37, "Doctors were not called in cases of ordinary illnesses; the family grandmother attended to those."

17. **(1) Comprehension/Supporting Details**
    Lines 30–34 state, "There were no dentists. When teeth became touched with decay or were otherwise ailing, the doctor knew of but one thing to do: he fetched his tongs and dragged them out."

18. **(2) Application**
    A modern-day physician would consider bloodletting and prescribing all-purpose medicines dangerous to a patient's health.

19. **(2) Extended Synthesis**
    With sentences like "It was a dreadful system, yet the death-rate was not heavy," which describes home remedies, the author uses subtle humor to make his point. The author also uses exaggeration to make situations appear worse than they really were. Much of his writing looked at life with humor.

20. **(2) Comprehension/Supporting Detail**
    In lines 21–22, the author states, "but it was safety that drew us all to Ted."

21. **(5) Comprehension/Supporting Details**
    The word *magician* is used figuratively to describe Ted's incredible skill in repairing fan belts.

22. **(3) Synthesis/Main Idea**
    Because Ted is concerned with avoiding traffic accidents, he would most likely urge a drunken driver not to drive.

23. **(4) Analysis/Supporting Details**
    The author does not mention registering the causes of traffic fatalities in the passage.

24. **(2) Synthesis/Linking Elements**
    The passage details Ted's commitment to serving his customers and for their safety. Therefore, you can conclude that Ted is a caring person.

25. **(1) Application**
    The author reveals Ted's character by describing his appearance, actions, physical surroundings, and relationships with people. A short story writer uses similar methods of characterization.

26. **(5) Synthesis/Tone**
    The informative tone of the passage is revealed in the facts and details explaining folk heroes and tall tales.

27. **(2) Analysis/Supporting Details**
    The author states in lines 1–4, "The heroes of the American frontier were superstrong, unflinchingly brave, and unusually keen— just as we would secretly like to be." The author assumes that the reader admires the traits of the hero, just as he does.

28. **(3) Application**
    As the first female astronaut, Sally Ride demonstrated her courage, intelligence, and physical strength—the attributes of the traditional American folk hero.

29. **(4) Comprehension/Supporting Details**
    The author defines the tall tale as "deliberate exaggeration" (line 12), which is a distinctive storytelling device.

30. **(2) Comprehension/Main Idea**
    Most of the supporting details in the second paragraph summarize a tall tale about a man and a mountain lion.

31. **(4) Analysis/Fact and Opinion**
    The biographical details in choices (1), (2), (3), and (5) are all factual statements that can be verified. Answer (4) is an opinion explaining a possible reason for a change in Lorca's poetic style.

32. **(3) Comprehension/Main Idea**
    The passage states that "Lorca's poetry is always wild and strange" and "There are mysterious places and unexplainable things and extraordinary events" (lines 12–15).

33. **(3) Application**
The authors state in the concluding paragraph that people tend to project their moods on the world around them. Therefore, they would probably believe that a sunny day seems gloomy to a depressed person.

34. **(2) Synthesis/Purpose**
The passage focuses on how Lorca's imagination is expressed in the subjects and the language of his poetry.

35. **(1) Analysis/Structure**
By using the pronoun *you* in the third paragraph, the authors directly address the reader. You, the reader, are asked to think about how your feelings affect the way you see the world. As a result, you can more closely identify with Lorca's perceptions in his poetry.

36. **(4) Extended Synthesis**
The authors reveal that in the years since Lorca's death in 1936, there has been a continued interest in his writings. The Spanish government may have killed him and banned his works, but his ideas live on.

37. **(2) Analysis/Style**
Mary Wilson insultingly calls Diana Ross "a scene-stealing, manipulative, ambitious prima donna" (lines 1–2). Mary Wilson's pointed remarks immediately catch the reader's attention.

38. **(4) Synthesis/Tone**
You can infer that the reviewer finds the book informative from such lines as, "[Wilson] manages to avoid making Ross the real star of the story by providing a wealth of information about the early days at Motown" (lines 32–35).

39. **(2) Analysis/Supporting Details**
Because Mary Wilson criticizes Diana Ross's self-centered and temperamental behavior, you can conclude that these actions were the source of the conflict between the two singers.

40. **(5) Comprehension/Main Idea**
The reviewer directly states the main idea of the third paragraph: "And Wilson's book is much more than an exposé. She manages to avoid making Ross the real star of the story by providing a wealth of information about the early days at Motown."

41. **(4) Comprehension/Supporting Details**
Dreamgirl is the title of Mary Wilson's book about The Supremes. All of the other choices are names of Motown bands listed in the passage.

Visual Nonfiction, pages 28–36

1. **(4) Comprehension/Supporting Details**
In lines 15–16 the author describes the "remarkable sets of art designer Herman Rosse."

2. **(1) Analysis/Style**
The author describes the "birth" of the monster and quotes Frankenstein's excited reaction. This is one of the most dramatic moments of the movie.

3. **(1) Synthesis/Purpose**
Most of the supporting details in the passage depict the scene in which Frankenstein creates the monster. Therefore, you can infer that the author's central purpose is to describe this scene.

4. **(3) Application**
Frankenstein is driven to create a human being asexually. Cloning is a technology that can do this.

5. **(4) Analysis/Structure**
The supporting details in the passage summarize the movie's plot—the sequence of events.

6. **(3) Analysis/Supporting Details**
The comparison of the opening scene to a fairy tale reflects the author's opinion. Other film critics might interpret this scene differently.

7. **(2) Comprehension/Supporting Details**
Lines 39–46 state, "Just as he [George] was about to jump off a bridge, however, Clarence materialized, jumped in first, and called for help. George instinctively jumped in to save him but refused to accept Clarence's subsequent explanation: 'I'm your guardian angel. I've come here to help you.'"

8. **(1) Application**
Just as three ghosts show Scrooge the joy of Christmas, so does Clarence show George how wonderful his life is.

9. **(2) Comprehension/Supporting Details**
Lines 9–10 state that Leopold and Loeb bludgeoned Bobby Franks to death.

10. **(4) Analysis/Style**
Logan is using this statement figuratively. Because he implies that he senses Leopold and Loeb's actual presence, he feels compelled to tell their story "honestly and effectively" (line 6).

11. **(2) Application**
Logan "writes about sensational murders, the ones that make tabloid headlines in their time and fascinate criminologists forever afterward" (lines 17–20). Lizzie Borden's ax murders fit into this category.

12. **(5) Comprehension/Supporting Details**
The reviewer directly states in lines 23–25, "Logan has a unique ability to climb inside the minds of his killers (or accused killers) and present their motives and feelings."

13. **(4) Analysis/Supporting Details**
Because Logan presents the "chronicled facts" (line 26) surrounding notorious crimes, you can infer that he conducts library research to find accurate background information.

14. **(4) Analysis/Structure**
The author lists symptoms, or effects, of stagefright, such as nausea and weak knees.

15. **(2) Comprehension/Supporting Details**
Lines 25–26 state, "Violinist Kato Havas wrote a book on it [stagefright]."

16. **(5) Application**
Many people experience the nervous symptoms associated with stagefright during an important job interview. Like an actor at an audition, the applicant is, in a sense, "onstage," since his performance is being judged by an audience—the interviewer.

17. **(1) Comprehension/Supporting Details**
Referring to the causes of stagefright, the author states, "Usually, however, it is Ego that takes the blame. Performers, like the rest of us, want to be admired for their work" (lines 31–33). In other words, a performer's ego, or self-esteem, depends on the admiration he or she receives. Therefore, you can conclude that a performer's stagefright usually stems from fear of disapproval.

18. **(3) Analysis/Supporting Details**
Reactions to stagefright include memory loss (a psychological symptom) and heart pounding (a physiological symptom). There is not sufficient evidence in the passage to support the other inferences.

19. **(2) Analysis/Figurative Language**
Descriptions of "vaulted ceilings" and "classical columns" (lines 5 and 9) suggest that the emergency center resembles a castle.

20. **(4) Comprehension/Supporting Details**
Lines 14–15 directly state, "For centuries the word hospital summoned up images of suffering and death."

21. **(1) Comprehension/Main Idea**
Lines 19–22 state, "The 1980s revolution in health care, spurred by new tools, attitudes and cures that prolong life, is matched by a similar revolution in architecture." This comparison is also the main idea of the second paragraph.

22. **(2) Application**
In the passage the authors seem enthusiastic about the choices available to today's patients. They can select comfortable, attractive facilities that specifically accommodate their health care needs. Therefore, they would probably recommend that a pregnant woman stay in a specialized women's hospital, a medical facility designed for women.

23. **(5) Analysis/Style**
The authors' writing style is highly descriptive: They use vivid images and colorful adjectives to detail the physical appearance and the atmosphere of hospitals. A magazine article about doctors' waiting rooms would also have a descriptive writing style if the authors' purpose was to make the reader visualize this setting.

24. **(4) Comprehension/Main Idea**
Like the theme of a novel or a play, the phrase "profound antiwar painting" best expresses a general message about the subject of the painting.

25. (1) Application
Because Pippin was wounded and disabled in the war, other disabled veterans would be most likely to find his artistic abilities inspirational. Pippin created paintings despite his severe physical handicaps.

26. (2) Comprehension/Supporting Details
Lines 6–8 state that Pippin "piled one coat of paint on top of another until at last it was thick with paint."

27. (4) Analysis/Style
Throughout the passage, the author recreates in words the appearance of Pippin's paintings. The vivid descriptions help the reader to imagine the pictures.

28. (2) Comprehension/Supporting Details
Lines 30–31 state that in each of Pippin's war paintings, "he showed the life of Black soldiers."

29. (3) Synthesis/Purpose
The author announces the place of the exhibit and comments on particular pieces. Therefore, you can infer that this article reviews the folk art exhibit.

30. (4) Comprehension/Main Idea
The author states in lines 1–3, "One of the wonderful things about folk art is it expresses an inner patience on the part of the artist." The author later refers to folk artists as "patient souls" (line 21). He develops this point through examples.

31. (2) Application
Folk art consists mainly of simple handicrafts. A marble sculpture is a more elaborate art form.

32. (5) Comprehension/Word in Context
The words *waves*, *seas*, and *aquarium* are the context clues suggesting that *aquatic* means something associated with water.

33. (2) Analysis/Style
To describe the whalebone etching, the author uses the phrases "touching piece" (lines 27–28) and "looks like a valentine to a lover" (lines 29–30). These descriptions convey an emotional tone.

Prose Fiction

Works written before 1920, pages 37–42

1. (2) Comprehension/Main Idea
The narrator states in lines 1–2, "Dorothea was in the reaction of a rebellious anger."

2. (3) Analysis/Figurative Language
Dorothea realizes here that the "paths of her young hope" (line 12)—the freedom she had as a girl—have disappeared. She is now a married woman who must live with the choices she has made.

3. (2) Analysis/Main Idea
You can infer from lines 20–25 that Dorothea once believed in her husband but is now disillusioned with him and confused about his place in her life.

4. (5) Synthesis
Dorothea would agree that married people can become like strangers because this has happened to her. She and her husband "walked apart" in "solitude" (line 15).

5. (4) Extended Synthesis
The entire passage reveals Dorothea's disappointment in her husband. The next-to-last sentence reveals Dorothea's thoughts: "Was it her fault that she had believed in him—had believed in his worthiness?—And what, exactly, was he?"

6. (2) Comprehension/Supporting Details
Hal and Ray are in a "big empty field" (lines 22–23).

7. (3) Application
Hal "got Nell Gunther in trouble," meaning that he got her pregnant (lines 15–16). Unwanted pregnancies are also a current social problem.

8. (4) Analysis/Figurative Language
Hal is speaking figuratively about asking Nell Gunther to marry him.

9. (5) Analysis/Style
The narrator uses descriptive language to make a "picture": His words "paint" a portrait of two men striking a pose against the background of the cornfield and the distant "red and yellow" hills.

10. **(3) Analysis/Supporting Details**

In lines 32–40, Hal tells Ray, "I know what everyone would say is the right thing to do, but what would you say? … Whatever you say, Ray, I'll do." Therefore, you can conclude that Hal respects Ray's opinion.

11. **(4) Extended Synthesis**

From the passage, it appears that Hal is under societal pressure to marry Nell, but does not want to. Since he did not wait for Ray to give his opinion, you can infer that societal pressure caused him to make the decision he did.

12. **(3) Analysis/Structure**

The narrator analyzes a cause-and-effect relationship: "the vicinity of Sleepy Hollow" (the cause) and "the prevalence of supernatural stories" (the effect).

13. **(2) Comprehension/Supporting Details**

Lines 6–7 state that "it [Sleepy Hollow] breathed forth an atmosphere of dreams and fancies."

14. **(5) Analysis/Supporting Details**

The "prevalence of supernatural stories" (line 2) in Sleepy Hollow suggests that the townspeople are superstitious.

15. **(3) Comprehension/Supporting Details**

Lines 20–23 state, "The chief part of the stories, however, turned upon the favorite spectre of Sleepy Hollow, the headless horseman."

16. **(2) Application**

The people of Sleepy Hollow would probably be most fascinated with a science fiction show, which would probably feature episodes about the supernatural and the occult and unexplainable phenomena.

17. **(2) Extended Synthesis**

Because Major Andre was a real person who was hanged during the 1700's, it makes the stories of the headless horseman more realistic.

18. **(4) Comprehension/Supporting Details**

Finding the murder weapon in a suspect's belongings would be the strongest evidence that he committed the crime.

19. **(1) Comprehension/Main Idea**

This response summarizes the plot details of the passage. The police officer questions Askenov about the merchant's murder.

20. **(3) Analysis/Style**

The ellipses (…) indicate the pauses in Askenov's statement. His dialogue about the murder weapon is punctuated with ellipses to show the interruptions in his speech resulting from nervousness. Lines 33–34 state, "Askenov wanted to answer, but he could not speak."

21. **(4) Application**

The police officer behaves like a prosecuting attorney because his intentions are to prove that a suspect is guilty of committing a crime.

22. **(2) Extended Synthesis**

The wife's dream foreshadows Askenov's imprisonment until he is an old man.

Works written between 1920 and 1960, pages 42–46

1. **(2) Analysis/Structure**

The narrator, Laurie's mother, explains how her son's behavior as a "nursery-school tot" (line 7) differs from his behavior as a kindergartner.

2. **(1) Comprehension/Main Idea**

In line 18 Laurie's mother asks, "How was school today?" The dialogue in the passage stems from this topic.

3. **(4) Analysis/Supporting Details**

None of Laurie's actions in the passage can be accurately described as "sweet."

4. **(2) Comprehension/Supporting Details**

Laurie's mother directly states that Laurie "left" while his father was still speaking.

5. **(4) Application**

A child psychologist is professionally trained to analyze the personalities of young children.

6. **(2) Extended Synthesis**

Laurie is both the innocent angel, as he sees himself, and the devil Charles. Laurie and Charles are the same person.

7. **(3) Analysis/Style**

In the second paragraph, the author's descriptive language reveals his admiration for Brother Nachin. For example, "He [Brother Nachin] carried himself like an athlete—gently but with authority." You can also infer that the author admires Brother Nachin's command of the English language and his "striking" appearance.

8. **(5) Comprehension/Supporting Details**
   In the introductory sentence of the passage, the author states, "I was sitting in church … "

9. **(2) Analysis/Figurative Language**
   Because Brother Nachin "was nearly six feet tall," he "was a giant among Puerto Ricans." (lines 5–6). Therefore, you can infer that the word "giant" is used figuratively to emphasize Brother Nachin's height.

10. **(1) Analysis/Supporting Details**
    In lines 14–15, the author tells Brother Nachin, " 'I'm still working at the same old job.' I frowned." This line of dialogue and the author's facial expression (a frown) suggest the author's unhappiness about his job.

11. **(3) Synthesis/Main Idea**
    The supporting details in the passage focus on Brother Nachin's role in helping the author to get a job in a bakery.

12. **(4) Extended Synthesis**
    The author sees a positive future for immigrants if they have a well-paying jobs. Brother Nachin's comment in lines 21–25 hints that the labor unions will insure good-paying jobs for the immigrant workers.

13. **(3) Comprehension/Supporting Details**
    Lines 10–12 state that "George thought of going to summer school; but the kids in his classes would be too young."

14. **(5) Synthesis/Main Idea**
    The narrator summarizes George's homelife, education, and financial situation.

15. **(1) Analysis/Supporting Details**
    Lines 18–19 state that George "had needs with the neighborhood girls, but no money to spend." You can conclude that George would like to earn money to pay for dates.

16. **(2) Comprehension/Supporting Details**
    The last sentence of the passage states that "most of the time he sat in his room."

17. **(5) Application**
    A career counselor would probably advise George to get his high school diploma because it would make him more employable.

18. **(4) Analysis/Style**
    Like a biography, the passage informatively profiles a person's life.

19. **(2) Extended Synthesis**
    Although George's character appears lazy and hides out in his home, he is ashamed that people will think less of him for leaving school. George wants to feel important.

Works written after 1960, pages 46–51

1. **(3) Analysis/Structure**
   The pronoun *I* in the story refers to Antonio Sousea, the narrator.

2. **(2) Analysis/Supporting Details**
   The passage states that the police officer's uniform cuffs were pulled over the black half-Wellingtons (lines 24–25). From this clue, you can infer that half-Wellingtons are boots.

3. **(2) Synthesis/Main Idea**
   The police officer says in line 54, "I don't like smart guys, Indians … " His derogatory statement implies a prejudice against Native Americans.

4. **(4) Synthesis/Supporting Details**
   Leon's hands are shaking, and Antonio's legs are quivering. These gestures show their nervousness.

5. **(2) Comprehension/Supporting Details**
   Antonio, the narrator, states in lines 33–35, "His voice was high-pitched and it distracted me from the meaning of the words."

6. **(4) Comprehension/Supporting Details**
   Lines 8–10 state that Aurora "continued to smite her forehead vigorously, as she always did when she was very upset … "

7. **(2) Comprehension/Main Idea**
   Emma asks her mother, "What's the point then?" Aurora replies, "Who will I ever … get now? … What man would want a grandmother?" (lines 45–47)

8. **(3) Analysis/Supporting Details**
   Line 44 state that Emma "understood a little and put out her arm." Therefore, you can infer that Emma is attempting to console her mother and is showing sympathy.

9. **(4) Analysis/Style**
   The dialogue conveys the emotions of a real fight.

10. **(2) Application**
Aurora's excessive display of emotions characterizes many actresses' performances in soap operas. Emma's pregnancy is not a horrible event, yet Aurora behaves as though it is.

11. **(1) Analysis/Supporting Details**
Squeaky knows that Cynthia's success results from hard work, but Cynthia gives the false impression that she never studies. Therefore, you can infer that Squeaky thinks that Cynthia is hypocritical.

12. **(2) Comprehension/Main Idea**
This answer paraphrases the main idea stated in the first sentence: "Now some people like to act like things come easy to them, won't let on that they practice."

13. **(3) Analysis/Structure**
Squeaky, the narrator, states in line 10 that Cynthia Proctor is her opposite. The passage details how the two characters are different.

14. **(3) Analysis/Figurative Language**
Squeaky says in lines 4–5 that she prances "like a rodeo pony" to keep her "knees strong." Squeaky is speaking figuratively to exaggerate the way she raises her knees.

15. **(5) Synthesis/Linking Elements of a Passage**
At three different points in the passage, Squeaky refers to her desire to be a good runner. In lines 3–5, she tells of "high-prancing" to keep her knees strong. In lines 21–22, she refers to her "early morning trots around the block." In the concluding sentence, Squeaky states, "And you can see me any time of the day practicing running." Her focus on running implies that Squeaky would like to be a track star.

16. **(1) Synthesis/Tone**
Throughout the passage, Squeaky pokes fun at Cynthia. The humorous tone of the passage stems from Squeaky's comic portrayal of Cynthia.

17. **(5) Comprehension/Supporting Details**
The narrator states in lines 9–10 that his father "came out to the garden and asked me to throw the ball to him."

18. **(4) Comprehension/Supporting Details**
The narrator states in line 12 that he threw the ball "clumsily."

19. **(1) Analysis/Style**
Literally, drowning means "suffocating by water." By using the word figuratively, the narrator emphasizes how it felt to have a mouthful of blood.

20. **(4) Synthesis/Main Idea**
Because almost half the passage details this incident, you can conclude that this event was the most important.

21. **(2) Analysis/Supporting Details**
Earlier in the passage, the mother and father quarreled because he refused to play catch with their son. You can infer that the father probably thinks his wife will become angry again if she finds out that the boy has been injured.

Poetry

pages 53–63

1. **(1) Synthesis/Tone**
The speaker's somber mood and his description of his mother's grief convey a feeling of sadness.

2. **(3) Analysis/Supporting Details**
The speaker says that he "left at once" (line 11) after his mother announced the news of his father's death. Therefore, you can conclude that he is going to attend his father's funeral.

3. **(3) Analysis/Supporting Details**
The speaker states in lines 4 and 5, "Sitting awake and alone/I worry the stewardess . . ." The speaker is implying that the stewardess senses that he is upset.

4. **(5) Synthesis/Main Idea**
The content of the poem centers around the feelings of a passenger on the way to his father's funeral.

5. **(2) Comprehension/Supporting Details**
"Would you like some coffee, sir?" and "How about a magazine?" are questions that a stewardess would most likely ask.

6. **(2) Extended Synthesis**
When the speaker is alone with his thoughts, he reflects on the fact that he's flying home to his father's funeral, and his father had never flown on a plane. Readers can identify with the speaker who just wants to be alone to reflect on his memories of his father.

7. **(4) Synthesis/Main Idea**
After the poet read his book, he states, "I fully felt the joy that was Lincoln's (line 18). From this concluding statement you can infer that the poet wrote the poem to explain how Lincoln inspired his love of reading.

8. **(5) Analysis/Structure**
Lines 2–4 describe how Lincoln read a book. Lines 6–16 compare and contrast the poet's approach to reading a book with Lincoln's.

9. **(2) Analysis/Supporting Details**
Line 2 states that "Lincoln walked many miles for a book." By walking a mile to another library instead of going to his neighborhood library, the poet was trying to imitate Lincoln.

10. **(1) Analysis/Style**
The image of the poet reading with "a little flashlight" corresponds to the image of Lincoln reading "before a bubbling kettle fireplace." Both images identify sources of light for reading.

11. **(3) Application**
Lincoln's psychological problems would probably not be taught at the grade-school level.

12. **(5) Analysis/Structure**
The first stanza describes a boy's impressions of his "Papa's" job.

13. **(3) Comprehension/Supporting Details**
The factory is unique because of the product it manufactures—miracles.

14. **(3) Analysis/Figurative Language**
Soot is compared to snow to describe the powdery texture of dust covering the factory.

15. **(2) Application**
A factory that produces miracles is a fantasy that would most likely be the subject of a science fiction story.

16. **(2) Analysis/Supporting Details**
The boss explains the economics of operating a business and the way he promotes his product.

17. **(1) Synthesis/Tone**
Throughout the poem, the speaker reveals and accepts the fact that he is not like other people and that he is alone.

18. **(4) Application**
Like the speaker, a soloist is set off by himself or herself even when performing with others.

19. **(5) Analysis/Supporting Details**
In lines 1–8, the speaker reveals how he is not like others in his responses to life's joys and sorrows.

20. **(2) Analysis**
The speaker states that even from childhood (line 9) that he did not feel or respond as others did. Although others might find his reactions strange, he understood that he reacted differently.

21. **(2) Extended Synthesis**
The information suggests that because the speaker had been orphaned early in life and then estranged from his adoptive father, he felt alone in the world.

22. **(5) Analysis/Supporting Details**
The speaker of the poem is "traveling through the dark." The taillights and parking lights on his car are turned on. Therefore, you can conclude that the event described in this poem occurs in the evening.

23. **(4) Analysis/Style**
The poet uses descriptive language to create images of the dead deer, the car, the setting, and the man's actions.

24. **(3) Analysis/Supporting Details**
Lines 16–18 state that the doe's "fawn lay there waiting,/alive, still, never to be born." The doe's belly was large because she was pregnant.

25. **(1) Synthesis/Tone**
The speaker shows his respect toward animals by stopping his car, inspecting the dead deer and thinking about her death, and then pushing her into the river.

26. **(2) Application**
Wildlife preservationists would be the most concerned with the treatment of deer.

27. **(4) Comprehension/Supporting Details**
Lines 1 and 2 state that the speaker is "Looking through boxes/in the attic."

28. **(3) Comprehension/Supporting Details**
Line 28 states, "I was happy."

29. **(5) Inferential Understanding/Main Idea**
    Lines 20–27 describe the boy's relationship with his pet dog named Tommy.

30. **(2) Analysis/Style**
    Connie Boswell, the singer, "was crippled, and sang/from a wheelchair" (lines 19–20). Despite her physical handicap, her voice turns "like a heel." This image is effective because of the sharp contrast.

31. **(4) Analysis/Figurative Language**
    The speaker compares her father's going to work to support and feed the family to a Native American who provides for his family by hunting.

32. **(2) Synthesis/Tone**
    Throughout the poem, the poet describes her father with a respectful tone, and implies that she sees himself as he sees himself, although others may not see him that way.

33. **(5) Analysis/Supporting Details**
    Had the father been living with a traditional Native American tribe, the first time he killed for food, he would have been considered an adult. He would have passed a rite of passage from boyhood to manhood, and the adults would have sung in his honor to mark the occasion.

34. **(1) Comprehension/Supporting Details**
    The following lines infer that the father was in the meat packing industry: Line 5, "He worked in the stockyards;" Line 6, "All his life he brought us meat;" Line 11, "and went to work in the packing house."

35. **(2) Synthesis/Organization**
    The daughter discusses the father's fantasizing his daily activities.

36. **(4) Extended Synthesis**
    In lines 21–24 she imagines that she sees the buffalo painted on her father's chest, and she fantasizes that his snores are buffalo grunts. She now mirrors the depiction of the father in lines 1–15.

37. **(4) Synthesis/Main Idea**
    In line 37, the young man exclaims, "O yes! I am poisoned." This is the central event described in the poem. From the supporting details you can conclude that his girlfriend is the murderess.

38. **(3) Analysis/Figurative Language**
    "Sick at the heart" is a figurative expression describing the young man's depression after he realizes his sweetheart has poisoned him.

39. **(1) Application**
    The details surrounding a murder would be an effective plot for a TV crime show.

40. **(2) Synthesis/Organization**
    Each of the first four stanzas consists of dialogue: The mother asks her son, Lord Randal, a question, and he responds.

41. **(3) Extended Synthesis**
    In the 13th and 14th centuries, the authorities didn't have the crime-solving technology that today's police use. Therefore, poisoning would probably have been unable to be proved.

42. **(2) Comprehension/Supporting Details**
    Line 1 identifies the setting—Hamelin Town.

43. **(4) Analysis/Main Idea**
    The supporting details in the stanza are all examples of how rats are destructive.

44. **(1) Analysis/Style**
    Like song lyrics, the sound of the rhyming words creates a musical effect.

45. **(3) Application**
    Like rats, cockroaches are annoying pests. They infest cities and pose a health hazard.

46. **(1) Extended Synthesis**
    The last part of the information, "let us keep our promises," implies that the council went back on its promise to pay the piper for ridding the town of its rats.

47. **(5) Comprehension/Supporting Details**
    Lines 7–8 state Mary's intentions: "To meet him [Warren] in the doorway with the news/And put him on his guard. 'Silas is back.'"

48. **(3) Analysis/Supporting Details**
    In lines 25–27 Warren states, "What help he [Silas] is there's no depending on./Off he always goes when I need him the most … " Therefore, you can infer that Warren believes Silas is unreliable.

49. **(5) Synthesis/Linking Elements**
Because Silas has helped Warren with haying, you can conclude that Warren is a farmer. References to a "doorway" (line 7), a "porch" (line 14), and "wooden steps" (line 16) suggest that the setting is a farmhouse.

50. **(4) Synthesis/Organization**
The poem contains the fictional elements of a short story—characterization, dialogue, conflict, and setting.

51. **(5) Extended Synthesis**
Although Warren is angry that Silas has returned, Mary reminds him that to Silas their place is his home. You can infer that Warren's anger will lessen.

52. **(2) Analysis/Figurative Language**
The word *falls* in line 3 is used figuratively to mean the soldier dies. The remaining lines interpret the significance of the soldier's death.

53. **(4) Synthesis/Tone**
The somber tone of the poem stems from the subject—the meaning of a soldier's death.

54. **(5) Comprehension/Supporting Details**
The poet compares death to autumn twice: "Life contracts and death is expected,/As in a season of autumn" (lines 1–2); and "Death is absolute and without memorial,/As in a season of autumn" (lines 8–9).

55. **(4) Synthesis/Organization**
The poet uses images suggesting death in nature to explain the inevitability of death in war.

56. **(5) Extended Synthesis**
When the poet's mother died, her death was a natural event; however, the loss of a young life in war is unnatural.

Drama

pages 65–79

1. **(5) Application**
Captain Davenport is a military lawyer, qualified to conduct a murder investigation. As a civilian, he would probably continue to practice law.

2. **(1) Analysis/Supporting Details**
Captain Davenport is methodical and well organized. He directly states his questions and takes notes.

3. **(2) Analysis/Inferences**
Private Wilkie has been rambling about the baseball team, a topic unrelated to the murder case. The stage direction effectively implies that Private Wilkie realizes this information is irrelevant.

4. **(3) Comprehension/Supporting Details**
After Captain Davenport introduces himself, Private Wilkie says, "Everybody knows that, sir" (lines 19–20).

5. **(3) Comprehension/Supporting Details**
Lenny states in lines 18–20, "all that she's [Meg's] done this whole year is work as a clerk for a dog food company."

6. **(4) Analysis/Supporting Details**
The playwright uses the word *slamming* to emphasize Lenny's anger and frustration with Meg.

7. **(1) Analysis/Style**
By recalling memories of Meg's adolescent behavior, Lenny convincingly shows that her attitude toward Meg can be traced to the past.

8. **(5) Synthesis/Main Idea**
When Babe realizes that Meg is not recording an album, she says, "Oh, shoot. I'm disappointed." (line 21) You can infer that Babe wishes that Meg actually were achieving fame as a singer. None of the other choices can be assumed from the passage.

9. **(2) Extended Synthesis**
When Lenny becomes furious that someone has taken bites from all of the pieces of her birthday candy, you assume that Meg is the guilty person. However, the additional information suggests that it wasn't Meg but Babe who ate the candy, and she probably hesitates before blaming Meg because she feels guilty.

10. **(4) Application**
Joe would probably respond to a want ad for a building contractor because of his previous experience as a builder, and because of the prestige and the salary associated with such a job.

11. **(3) Analysis/Supporting Details**
The stage directions state in line 28 that Joe "has risen from his bed." Therefore, you can infer that the scene takes place in a bedroom.

12. **(2) Comprehension/Supporting Detail**
In Joe's concluding dialogue about his daughter's financial support, he says, "Don't you think I have a little contempt for myself?"

13. **(1) Analysis/Supporting Details**
Because Joe "was a big operator fifteen years ago" (lines 1–3), he is unwilling to accept jobs that he considers a demotion.

14. **(5) Analysis/Structure**
The stage directions in parentheses explain Joe's gestures.

15. **(5) Analysis/Figurative Language**
Jack is using a figure of speech to exaggerate the effects of Willie's speech on his listeners. Their brain cells break down because Willie "tell[s] 'em too much" information (line 25).

16. **(4) Analysis/Style**
Sadie repeatedly uses the word "hell," calls Willie "a sucker," and describes the voters in a tactless manner.

17. **(4) Analysis/Supporting Details**
In this scene Willie is portrayed as naïve and inexperienced. He stands about "aimlessly" (line 14) and shows no practical knowledge of how to conduct a winning political campaign.

18. **(2) Application**
Sadie would probably suggest a revivalist preacher's sermon because it would "stir 'em up", as she suggests. She believes that Willie should excite the voters, not bore them.

19. **(2) Analysis/Supporting Details**
Willie asks Jack's opinion about the campaign. You can infer from their dialogue that Jack is an advisor to Willie.

20. **(5) Extended Synthesis**
Willie in the passage is a naïve and inexperienced politician and his advisors critique his speeches. You can infer that in order to win, he learned how to give speeches that excite the voters.

21. **(1) Analysis/Main Idea**
When she says in lines 25–26, "I know, but … there's some things he hasn't given me," Lottie reveals that her childlessness is the major disappointment in her marriage.

22. **(3) Analysis/Supporting Details**
When Lottie criticizes Morris, Cora says, "Morris is nice to you. You've got no right to complain" (lines 19–20). Cora sides with Morris throughout most of the scene.

23. **(2) Comprehension/Supporting Details**
Lottie says in line 10 that Morris claims "the walk helps his digestion."

24. **(2) Analysis/Supporting Details**
Since Cora was unaware of Lottie's desire to have children, you can infer that Lottie had concealed this feeling from her sister.

25. **(5) Application**
A marriage counselor is professionally trained to help couples, like Lottie and Morris, who have problems.

26. **(3) Analysis/Style**
This stage direction marks the change in Cora's attitude toward Lottie. Cora has misjudged Lottie's feelings because she never recognized Lottie's disappointment.

27. **(2) Comprehension/Supporting Details**
When Elizabeth starts to cry in line 19 and when she begs Emily to do her a favor, she feels partly responsible for hurting the boy's feelings and damaging her friendship with Inez.

28. **(3) Analysis/Supporting Details**
When Emily tells her mother that "I'll call Leo and see what he says." (lines 35–36), she suggests that she needs her boyfriend's approval.

29. **(1) Analysis/Supporting Details**
In order to make her mother stop crying, Emily will probably agree to go to the dance.

30. **(5) Application**
An eighteen- or twenty-year-old who is dating would feel similar pressure if a parent made a similar request.

31. **(2) Extended Synthesis**
The information suggests that Emily fails to consider the feelings of the boy. Her pretending to be ill rather than telling the boy the truth is insensitive of his feelings.

32. **(4) Comprehension/Supporting Details**
Blanche states in lines 16–18, "Mr. Graves is the high school superintendent—he suggested I take a leave of absence."

33. **(2) Analysis/Structure**
Nervously tamping cigarette (line 15) and *She drinks quickly* (line 20) describe gestures.

34. **(3) Application**
Blanche admits in lines 15–16, "I was on the verge of lunacy, almost." She should probably seek the advice of a psychiatrist to help her cope with her nervousness and exhaustion.

35. **(4) Analysis/Figurative Language**
Blanche says in lines 29–31, "But you—you've put on some weight, you're just as plump as a little partridge!"

36. **(2) Analysis/Supporting Details**
Blanche's order to Stella to "stand up" reveals her bossy behavior.

37. **(4) Extended Synthesis**
The information refers back to the beginning of the passage and Stella's impression that her sister has problems that may have forced her to give up her job.

38. **(5) Comprehension/Supporting Details**
Algernon reacts to Jack's announcement of his marriage proposal by saying in lines 8–9, "I thought you had come up for pleasure? … I call that business."

39. **(4) Analysis/Supporting Details**
Algernon seems to have very strong opinions about everything he and Jack discuss.

40. **(2) Comprehension/Supporting Details**
JACK puts out his hand to take a sandwich (lines 25–26) and *advancing to table and helping himself* (lines 38–39) both describe Jack's movements.

41. **(4) Application**
Algernon probably would offend socially conservative people, like those mentioned in the other choices, with his opinions on marriage.

42. **(4) Extended Synthesis**
Algernon, who ridicules marriage and romance throughout the passage, must have found someone who changed his views.

43. **(3) Comprehension/Supporting Details**
Dunyasha says that the time is "nearly two" (line 11). You know that it is 2:00 A.M. because the stage directions state that the "sun will soon rise" (line 3).

44. **(2) Comprehension/Supporting Details**
Lopakhin says in lines 16–18, "Came here on purpose to meet them at the station, and then overslept … "

45. **(4) Analysis/Main Idea**
Lopakhin's conversation focuses on his memories of the "sweet-tempered" (line 24) Lyubov Andreyevna. The details in the dialogue are associated either directly or indirectly with an incident he recalls about her kindness.

46. **(1) Analysis/Figurative Language**
The sentence immediately following this figure of speech suggests what Lopakhin meant: "I may be rich, I've made a lot of money, but if you think about it, analyze it, I'm a peasant through and through" (lines 38–40). In Lopakhin's comparison, "pig" refers to his peasant background, and "pastry shop" refers to the wealthy class.

47. **(5) Analysis/Structure**
The playwright states the month and the time of day and details about the place in which the dramatic action will occur.

48. **(2) Extended Synthesis**

    Because Lopakhin reveals that he was born a peasant to whom the owner once said, "Don't cry, little peasant," you can infer that the wealthy owner, Lyubov Andreyevna, and her friends resent losing their family estates to one born in a lower class.

49. **(2) Analysis/Figurative Language**

    Proctor says in line 55 "I sold my friends," referring to other citizens who refused to sign confessions and held to their beliefs to death.

50. **(1) Application**

    A prisoner of war who faced torture and other punishments by captors who use force to obtain false confessions would face a situation similar to Proctor's.

51. **(3) Comprehension/Supporting Details**

    In lines 33–34, Proctor states, "I confess to God, and God has seen my name on this!" Also, in lines 43–44, he says, "God does not need my name nailed upon the church!"

52. **(1) Analysis/Supporting Details**

    Throughout the passage, Danforth keeps asking Proctor to hand him the signed paper. Most of Danforth's lines are cut off by Proctor's refusals.

53. **(5) Analysis/Supporting Details**

    You can infer when Proctor says that he has sold his friends that he doesn't want them to see that he signed a confession; therefore, you can conclude that he is not telling the truth in the confession.

54. **(4) Extended Synthesis**

    The information explains the time in which the playwright wrote the play and the events with which he compared Proctor's trial. Like the people brought before the government panel in the 1950s, Proctor had to decide how to act with integrity: he couldn't betray his friends to save himself.